LANDSCAPE OF THE BODY

BY JOHN GUARE

★

★

DRAMATISTS
PLAY SERVICE
INC.

This play is for

Adele Chatfield-Taylor

LANDSCAPE OF THE BODY was first produced by William Gardner at the Academy Festival Theatre, in Lake Forest, Illinois, in July, 1977. It was directed by John Pasquin; the settings were by John Wulp; costumes were by Laura Crow; and the lighting was by Jennifer Tipton. The stage mechanics were by Robert Giffen; the production pianists were Rod Derefinko and William Snyder; and the stage manager (in both Lake Forest and New York) was Steven McCorkle. The cast, in order of appearance, was as follows:

BETTY	Shirley Knight
CAPTAIN MARVIN HOLAHAN	F. Murray Abraham
ROSALIE	Peg Murray
RAULITO	Richard Bauer
BERT	Paul McCrane
DONNY	Anthony Marciona
JOANNE	Alexa Kenin
MARGIE	Bonnie Deroski
MASKED MAN	Jay Sanders
DURWOOD PEACH	Rex Robbins
DOPE KING OF PROVIDENCE	Jay Sanders
BANK TELLER	Jay Sanders

4

LANDSCAPE OF THE BODY was then presented in New York City, by Joseph Papp at the Public Theatre (New York Shakespeare Festival) on October 12, 1977. It was directed by John Pasquin; the settings and costumes were by Santo Loquasto; lighting was by Jennifer Tipton; musical arrangements and incidental music were by Wally Harper; and the associate producer was Bernard Gersten. The pianist was Rod Derefinko. The cast, in order of appearance, was as follows:

BETTY	Shirley Knight
CAPTAIN MARVIN HOLAHAN	F. Murray Abraham
ROSALIE	Peg Murray
RAULITO	Richard Bauer
BERT	Paul McCrane
DONNY	Anthony Marciona
JOANNE	Alexa Kenin
MARGIE	Bonnie Deroski
MASKED MAN	Raymond J. Barry
DURWOOD PEACH	Remak Ramsay
DOPE KING OF PROVIDENCE	Raymond J. Barry
BANK TELLER	Raymond J. Barry

The play takes place on a ferry to Nantucket and in Greenwich Village.

Music and lyrics for all songs are by John Guare.

Landscape of the Body

*The deck of a ferry boat sailing from Hyannisport to
Nantucket. A woman sitting writing notes on the deck.
She is bundled up in layers of clothes against the cool.
She has shopping bags around her feet. When she finishes
one note, she rolls it into a cylinder and inserts it into a
bottle she takes out of the shopping bags. She seals the
bottle and tosses it overboard. She watches it go. She
begins another.*

*A man is watching her after a while. He is heavily dis-
guised. False eyeglasses and nose. Muffler wrapped high.
Hat pulled down. He carries a little suitcase.*

MAN. That's the Kennedy compound over there. I bought a postcard at the bus station in Hyannisport and the postcard tells you
whose house is who. (*Proffers it. She looks at it briefly. Looks at
the shore. Resumes her note writing.*) That house is Teddy Kennedy's and that house was where Jack lived and that house is where
the parents lived and that house is where the sister Eunice lived
and that house is where the sister Jean lived and that house—the
postcard seems not to match up to reality. I get them all mixed up
now, it's been so long. Empty rooms. Open windows. White curtains blowing out. (*She looks up. Tosses another bottle over.
Watches it go.*) I won a contest in grammar school knowing the
names of the Dionne Quintuplets. I could rattle them off. Emilie.
Annette. See I can't even remember. Yvonne. And the worst is
nobody remembers the Dionne Quintuplets. You tell young people,
younger than we are, about the Dionne Quintuplets and they don't
know who you're talking about.
WOMAN. Emilie was the left handed one. Emilie was the only left
handed Dionne Quintuplet. What was the name of the doctor who
delivered the Dionne Quintuplets?

MAN. Dr. Dafoe.

WOMAN. Dr. Dafoe.

MAN. We could have a marriage made in heaven sharing information like that.

WOMAN. I'm not in the market.

MAN. I went down to Washington in 1960 for Kennedy's inauguration. They were selling at the Union Station an entire set of dishes of China and every plate was a different Kennedy. The big meat platter was Poppa Joe. The other cake platter had Momma Rose on it. JohnJohn and Caroline were on little bread and butter plates. You're so open to talk to. Generally on trips of this nature—three hour ferry trips from the mainland to an island—you begin talking to your fellow ship mates desperately leaping into conversational gambits, reduced to buying dusty postcards of abandoned compounds of families who once made all the difference in America. I begin talking and you pick right up on it. We could have a marriage made in heaven. We can talk. I think that's why marriages fail. People can't talk. People fight to have something to talk about. People kill each other, say, because the words won't come into place. I think of murder, say, as a sentence that did not make it through the computer up here in the head. If people had a better grasp of language, of syntax, of the right word, of being understood, you'd hear that crime rate, you'd see that homicide rate plunge like those bottles you're tossing over . . . would they be sentences you'd be writing on that piece of paper? (*She tosses another bottle over.*) What attracted you to me first? My confidence inspiring voice? My ability to select the proper word out of the autumn air? A poll said what women notice most in men was their butts. Is that it? You liked my ass? Is that what attracted you to me? Are the polls right? My confidence is in bad disrepair and needs all the propping up it can beg, borrow or infer.

WOMAN. I saw you getting on the boat. I wondered if you were in disguise. I said to myself, is this a masquerade cruise? Then I thought this is a man with a facial cancer and his face has been removed and replaced by a necessary false nose to disguise the two gaping holes under there. A false mustache to cover the missing upper lip. False eyebrows to cover the grafted skin around the eyeballs which still function or he'd be tapping a white cane around this deck. He walks with a steady stride. No, I won't have to be yelling Man Overboard. It's a disguise.

8

MAN. You recognized me?

WOMAN. Captain Marvin Holahan Sixth Precinct Homicide. (*The man pulls off his disguise.*)

HOLAHAN. What did you write in that note? A confession? (*She throws sheets of small papers into the wind. They blow away. She pours bottles overboard.*)

WOMAN. A confession. A full confession. I wrote down everything that happened. And it's all gone. There it goes! There's your case. (*They face each other. The lights go down on them. They each take off their coats. The light is harsh in this interrogation room. She sits down in a chair. He circles her. He shines a desk lamp in her eyes.*)

VOICE. Flashback. Five months before. Marvin Holahan. Betty Yearn. Sixth Precinct. New York City. A spring day. Easter Sunday. Vernal equinoxes. The sun and moon cross each other's path.

BETTY. I don't see how you can ask me these questions.

HOLAHAN. Easy.

BETTY. At this point in my life in history you could ask me these questions.

HOLAHAN. The kid is dead.

BETTY. I cannot cannot cannot—draw underlines under the cannot—cannot cannot cannot—six negatives make a positive—cannot understand—

HOLAHAN. How I can ask you these questions?

BETTY. How you can ask me these questions—

HOLAHAN. Lady, I'm not talking simple child-battering.

BETTY. The kid is dead. The kid is dead. You leave out the fact it's my kid.

HOLAHAN. Decapitation, Betty.

BETTY. My son is dead. My boy is dead. My kid killed. Not *the* kid. My kid.

HOLAHAN. The head chopped off, Betty. That's not Family Court. Chopped off heads are not referrals to Family Counseling. That goes beyond child battering.

BETTY. Not *the* kid. *My* kid. *My* kid.

HOLAHAN. You and your boy friend didn't say my kid when you got out the hack saw. You must've said, oh, let me guess: you little bastard.

BETTY. I'm not going to throw up.

9

HOLAHAN. What did your kid see, Betty, that you had to chop his head off?

BETTY. If I throw up, it's like you win. You're not going to win.

HOLAHAN. Where's the boy's father?

BETTY. I haven't seen him in years.

HOLAHAN. Maybe the boy's father did it in revenge against you?

BETTY. Strangers don't do revenge. The father didn't even know where we live. I feel like I'm standing in that corner over there watching me, and if I try hard enough I can switch the dial and I'll see me on another channel. I'd like a laugh track around my life. I'd like a funny theme introducing my life. I'm standing right over there in that corner watching me.

HOLAHAN. Was your boy homosexual?

BETTY. He's fourteen, for God's sake.

HOLAHAN. Lady, we got bodies coming in here don't even live to be fourteen. Their ages never get off the fingers of two hands.

BETTY. There's a whole series of homosexual murders going on down there at Christopher Street. Maybe the kid was into something. I don't think so. Don't those murders involve decap—the heads off . . .

HOLAHAN. How do you know about that?

BETTY. Is that the clue that gives myself away? I read the papers. I hear on the street. Did you follow up that clue? Why did you drag me in here? I'm supposed to be out there, mourning, weeping—

HOLAHAN. Betty, I'm trying to be kind. If you're embarrassed confessing to such a heinous crime, you want me to get Sergeant Lorraine Dean down here? There ain't nothing Lorraine hasn't heard. She's a good woman, a good listener, heavy in the ankles, platinum blonde, a nice soft bosom that I swear has got seconal and libriums in. She'd hold you and rock you in the cradle of the deep and she'll sing "I'm confessing that I love you . . ." She'll sing that and make it easy for you to talk about what you did and get you help. She's got a nice voice Lorraine does. She could've made it big in the show biz department were it not for her tragedy in the ankle department. Should I get Lorraine down here and you can tell her all? You want Lorraine? "I just found joy. I'm as happy as a baby boy. With another brand new choo choo toy when I marry my Lorraine!" Betty? You could tell me too? There's nothing hadn't been poured into these ears. I'm taking courses at

10

NYU nights in psychology. Things like you did happen all the time. We even had a spot quiz last week on a woman, went into a deep depression, drowned her two kids. Two! You just did one. Imagine how she feels. But they were infants. And she drowned them. I can't wait to ask my teacher about decapitation. You might help me get an honors. I might do a paper on you. Most infanticides are drownings or smotherings or an occasional throwing off a bridge . . .

BETTY. I remember when I was a little kid at the end of the McCarthy hearings when Joe McCarthy was destroying human lives, this great lawyer—

HOLAHAN. Welch. Joseph Welch.

BETTY. Stood up and said to McCarthy Is there no such thing as human decency? And that question shocked everybody and destroyed Joe McCarthy.

HOLAHAN. I'll tell you that great lawyer Welch after that made a film for Otto Preminger called *Anatomy of A Murder* starring James Stewart and Lee Remick. Is there no such thing as human decency left?

BETTY. Is there no such thing as human decency left?

HOLAHAN. A damn good little question.

BETTY. Will I get off to go to my son's funeral?

HOLAHAN. Is Otto Preminger filming it?

BETTY. Am I booked? What's up? Do I go to my son's funeral?

HOLAHAN. Did you kill him?

BETTY. Do I get off for the funeral?

HOLAHAN. Say yes, beautiful Betty, and there's no place you can't go.

BETTY. I want my boy buried in Bangor, Maine with his grandparents and his aunts and his uncles. I want him buried in Bangor with my father, with my sister Rosalie. Where I'll be buried when I die. I want him there. I want him out of New York.

HOLAHAN. You think it's fair to be at the funeral when you caused the funeral?

BETTY. I'm sorry, Your Honor, Mr. Kangaroo Court. I missed his death.

HOLAHAN. I keep thinking you were there.

BETTY. What is my motive? I cannot believe I am a suspect in my own son's death. I am supposed to be comforted. I am supposed to be held and allowed to cry and not made to feel . . . there's

11

no insurance. I am no beneficiary. I cannot believe. I don't kill my own flesh and blood. I don't kill me. If I wanted to kill him, I would've killed me along with him. I don't kill me. I am here. Am I a car? A car you have to pull over to the side of the road and give a ticket to? You have to torture a certain number of people a day? Is this torture a routine formality? My boy is dead. I would like to grieve.

HOLAHAN. When did you come to New York?

BETTY. Two years ago.

HOLAHAN. Why?

BETTY. To get my sister.

HOLAHAN. Where is your sister now?

BETTY. My sister's dead.

HOLAHAN. Let me get this straight. You came to New York two years ago to get your dead sister.

BETTY. She was not dead at the time.

HOLAHAN. You came to New York two years ago alone to get your sister.

BETTY. Not alone. With Bert.

HOLAHAN. Bert? Bert?

BETTY. My kid.

HOLAHAN. The one you killed. Ah, yes, that Bert. (*A redhead appears out of the dark. She's very tough, very blowsy. A good sport. Her name is Rosalie.*)

ROSALIE. They're getting you for your life style, kid. They can't stand it that you got the life style of the future and they're stuck here in their little precincts.

BETTY. I'm being prosecuted for my life style. You can't stand it that I got the life style of the future and you're stuck here in your little precinct. (*Rosalie embraces Betty and comforts her. Rosalie goes back into the dark.*)

HOLAHAN. Bert's body was found yesterday afternoon floating off an abandoned pier at the bottom of Charles Street in a particularly seedy part of Greenwich Village. The boy's head was found floating close by. No signs of sexual molestation. But the boy was not killed there. The murder took place someplace else. The body was taken and dumped off this abandoned pier notorious for sexual pickups between members shall we say of the same sex and for the exchange of narcotic goods exchanged between people so spaced out they don't know what sex they are. From the boy's school pass, we find where he lives on Christopher Street, a notorious street in the self-same Greenwich Village. We find evidence in the boy's apartment where he lives with his mother, we find evidences of blood in his own home. In the bathroom. The boy was murdered and decapitated in the bathroom of his own legal abode. The mother lived there with the boy. The mother is a hotsytotsy we find out. The mother works in porno films.

BETTY. Soft core.

HOLAHAN. *Do Me Do Me Do Me Till It Falls Off* does not sound soft core to me. *Leather Sheets* does not sound soft core to me. Vaginal penetration recorded in medical detail by a sixteen millimeter camera owned by Mafia people does not sound soft core to me.

BETTY. That wasn't me in all of them. My sister worked in porno films. I was finishing up a contract she had made shortly before her death.

HOLAHAN. And when you appear on *What's My Line?* How do you sign in, please?

BETTY. I work in a travel agency.

HOLAHAN. A fake travel agency. *(Raulito, a Cuban in a trench coat, appears out of the dark.)*

RAULITO. Honeymoon Holidays was not fake.

HOLAHAN. Closed down for selling fraudulent trips—

RAULITO. It don't harm nobody to start off a marriage with a good honeymoon. *(Raulito goes back into the dark. Betty takes pills out of her pocket. Holahan knocks them out.)*

HOLAHAN. No junkie shit here, baby.

BETTY. They're *Tums* for the tummy, asshole. I don't want to throw up. If I do not throw up, it will somehow prove to me that I am not on your level, that I possess a strength, am the proud possessor of a dignity—

HOLAHAN. And yet Miss Dignity seems to appear in these loops. We raided Dirty Mort's on Forty Second Street. We ran the loops. I remembered your face from the loops when they brought you in. I had long said to myself what kind of person would allow another human being to urinate on her while a Mafia run camera was whirring away. Little did I think, Miss Life Style of the Future, I would have the honor of having met you. As you see, I am a movie buff. Those films. These films. This doesn't look like anybody's sister to me. This looks coincidentally like you. Or

13

maybe it's Gene Kelly in outtakes from *Singin' in the Rain*? What kind of human being allows herself to be treated in this way? I hate you, baby.

BETTY. No shit, Dick Tracy. I thought this was a love story.

HOLAHAN. When I was a kid my parents chained me to the piano so I'd play. I was a fat kid, too, so the chains had a double purpose. The pressure of them would stop me eating and force me to play. I eat, baby. I eat the right amounts and I am thin and I play the piano very well. And I also know all about family hatred. I know that families are there to learn your deepest secrets and betray you with their intimacy. Your kid must've found out too much about you. Your kid, I'm beginning to see, cramped your style. Of course! Every kid thinks his mother is the Virgin Mary, for Christ's sake, and one day your kid sees the films you work in when you're not in the fake travel agency. I get it! And I find it a fantastic fact that a woman who gives head in twenty five cent loops should be in here for taking head. To get rid of the son's head that contained the eyes that saw her life.

BETTY. Are you nuts?

HOLAHAN. Because his eyes turned into these Mason jars preserving the disgust at what you had become.

BETTY. I want out of here! (*Bangs on doors.*) That's not me in those films. That's my sister.

HOLAHAN. Oh sure. Your sister. Bring her in here. Testify for you.

BETTY. She's dead.

HOLAHAN. When?

BETTY. A year ago, last October. (*Raulito appears.*)

RAULITO. Is that what happened to you?

BETTY. She was walking on Hudson Street. (*Rosalie appears.*)

ROSALIE. I was just walking on Hudson Street.

BETTY. A cyclist hit her.

HOLAHAN. And Raulito?

BETTY. He's dead. (*Raulito and Rosalie go in the black.*)

HOLAHAN. You're a terrific dame to know. All the people connected to you via the avenue of blood die in one year. Maybe I'll go to Bangor, Maine and dig your sister up.

BETTY. I'm really grateful to you.

HOLAHAN. *The Grateful Dead.* The noted rock group.

BETTY. I am alive, detective. Because I am, I was going crazy from my kid's murder. When they came and told me the kid was dead, they could've fit me for a strait jacket at the same time they were fitting him for a shroud. You have actually taken my mind off it. My loathing for you replaces my grief. I mean, my fury is real. You're nuts.

HOLAHAN. Do you deny you made golden shower films where people urinated on you?

BETTY. That was my sister.

HOLAHAN. Oh, this is one of those movies where there's a good twin and an evil twin.

BETTY. You got movies on the brain. It must make life easy for you. You can just put anything you want into a movie and that explains everything.

HOLAHAN. One good twin. One bad twin. Was it the good twin or the bad twin who made those animal films? *Barnyard Bimbo. Six With a Pig.* An alleged human being has sex with a German shepherd. Is that the sister? It looks a hell of a lot like the good twin sitting right here in her little Mary Janes and golden braids.

BETTY. I did it for the money.

HOLAHAN. Of all the motives, that still has to be my favorite motive. I did it for the money.

BETTY. My sister was in the hands of the mob. She owed them money. She was a junkie. They forced me to make the films to work off the bread she owed them for smack.

HOLAHAN. After "I did it for the money" my next favorite motive is the Mob made me do it. Get the Mob. The Mob did this, the Mob did that. The Mob must be pretty busy. That's some pretty busy Mob. My heart goes out to the Mob more and more every day. Nothing better than having a convenient fall guy. I'm sorry Betty. I look to the family. I go right to the scene of the crime between those shapely gams. The family, Betty.

BETTY. You're a class act, detective. Detective Marvin Holahan. *Detective That's Entertainment Parts One and Two and Three and Four.* What are you? Some faggot out to get me because—

HOLAHAN. I know everything about you.

BETTY. You don't know nothing about me except I posed for some sleazy pictures and who cares. But I know about you. They chained you to a piano so you wouldn't eat and you would play. And you do both and you're a good boy. A lot of things happened to me, but nobody ever chained me to a piano and you know what?

15

I didn't throw up. I can look you right in the eye. I didn't throw up. I won. (*The interrogation room goes into dark. Lights up on Rosalie. A piano swings into view. Music plays at the piano. She sings to us in the audience. She's really good-natured, has a swell voice, moves like a stripper.*)
ROSALIE.

>Hey stay a while*
>In the crook of my arms
>All you got to do is
>Look in my arms
>And you'll see Home Sweet Home
>I'll invest in a doormat
>Hey Home Sweet Home
>We'll test the mattress
>Our arms are sinuous
>All performances are continuous
>Hey Stay a While
>Feel the smile in my arms
>And the smile's in my arms
>All for you
>Sit back/Relax
>Cool brow/Tension slacks
>Hey stay a while
>My arms are filled with
>What the whole world lacks
>Hey Stay a While

Being dead is not the worst thing in the world. Is there life after death? I dare ask the question: Is there life before death. The good thing about being dead is at least you know where you stand. You have one piece of information in life and you think life means this. Then you get a new piece of info and everything you knew means something else. The scary thing about death is how comfortable it is. Finally giving into the drowning. Life was always wriggling out of my hands like a fish you thought you had all hooked and ready to pop in the pan. Was there ever a day I didn't at one point say, "Hey, when will life end?" Flashback! A new scene starring the boy who would soon be murdered. (*Bert, a fourteen year old kid, swaggers on. He has ear phones on. He dances on to silent music.*) This scene you are about to see contains information completely

---

* Music for this song appears at end of playbook.

unknown to the boy's mother, my sister. Information unknown to Captain Marvin Holahan of the Sixth Precinct Homicide. Those two people in the course of their lives never learned the information you are about to receive right now. This scene takes place in the Parthenon. Not the one in Greece that's the cradle of all civilization. Hell, baby, I'm talking the Parthenon Luncheonette on West Eleventh Street and Bleecker in Greenwich Village. This scene takes place four weeks before this boy, my nephew, will be murdered. (*A booth and table and chairs come in. Bert sits in the booth. His arm around one of the girls. Another boy, Donny, has his sleeves rolled up wearing a lot of wristwatches. The girls lean forward. The kids are roughly twelve, thirteen, fourteen.*)

BERT. It's so easy.

DONNY. Easy he says.

BERT. You stand on Christopher Street.

DONNY. I got to wait in the tub.

BERT. Pretty soon the guy stops.

DONNY. The tub gets cold. You got a cold ass waiting in the tub.

BERT. You noticed him cause he's walked back and forth a few times looking at you.

DONNY. All the things a tub can be. A coffin. I pretend I'm in a coffin.

JOANNE. Does he look at you like you're a girl?

DONNY. I pretend I'm in a boat.

JOANNE. Do they really look fruity?

BERT. Sometimes they're in cars. Not fruity cars, but Pontiacs. Oldsmobiles.

JOANNE. Fruits driving Pontiacs?

DONNY. I pretend I'm in a car.

MARGIE. I could see a Chevrolet. Chevrolets are fruity.

BERT. Not the '65 Chevy, Joanne. Holy-shit, Joanne, I look at you sometimes and I say—

JOANNE. It was Margie who said it.

BERT. You were looking at her, agreeing with her.

JOANNE. Don't get mad at me. I'm sorry, Bert?

BERT. I don't like the two of you hanging around together. She's dragging you down. We all got to protect each other. Make each other better. Margie's dragging you down.

JOANNE. She's not cheap.

MARGIE. I only felt cheap once in my life. Charlie Ebbermann said he'd give me ten cents to let him touch me in the cloakroom. This is the fifth grade. The sixth grade. So I do. Big deal. Then I hear later, Charlie Ebbermann is paying a girl from the public school a quarter to take out her glass eye and let him look in. I saw him and I said Look, Ebbermann, you can take your dime back and I threw it at him.

BERT. (Calls.) Hey, could we get a coke or something? A toasted bran?

DONNY. Bert brings the fruit upstairs. His mother's away. He leads them into the bathroom. I'm happy cause I can finally get out of the fucking tub. I hear the voices behind the shower curtain. I make sure the shower curtain's shut. I see the fruit's shadow on the shower curtain. I leap out of the tub and bang the guy on the head with the monkey wrench. He don't know what hit him.

BERT. I pull the watch off. Take the wallet. We roll 'em to the door. Push 'em out in the hall. We piss in the corner.

DONNY. Piss on the guy.

BERT. Then I knock on the door next door. Mrs. Pantoni, I tell her, there's another drunk broke in. He peed on the floor. I spill some wine on him. She calls the cops. The cops come and clear the guy out.

MARGIE. They don't ever report you?

BERT. You don't have big ears, but you're a real dumbo, Margie. I don't want you hanging around with her, Joanne.

JOANNE. I got to have some friends, Bert.

BERT. You got me.

JOANNE. You swear?

BERT. (Arm around Joanne.) Who they gonna report? Some fairy tries to pick up a fourteen year old?

JOANNE. All that ticking. Your arm is so noisy.

DONNY. You have all the fun. I got to stick in the tub. You wait in the tube for a while. You see how much fun it is in a fucking tub.

BERT. Some fairy in a Chevrolet with Jersey plates is gonna pick you up. I want to make some money, not scare 'em away.

DONNY. That's right. I'd scare 'em away. (Makes a face.)

JOANNE. Let me wind your watches? You read in the papers today about the lady in Forest Hills who died and they couldn't figure out how she died? She was healthy. Well, you know how she died?

18

BERT. Donny hit her over the head with his monkey.

DONNY. That's right. I hit her over the head with my monkey.

MARGIE. Would you let her tell her story?

BERT. (Calls.) You burning that bran muffin?

JOANNE. She had this beautiful beehive hairdo that she wore. Really intricate. Curls. Upswept. Spit curls. And she didn't want to damage it because her hairdo was really a work of art. *Hairdo Magazine* was considering her for a feature. And she kept spraying her hairdo with hair spray so her hairdo wouldn't get hurt when she went to sleep at night and you know what happened? In Forest Hills, Queens, they traced black widow spiders escaped and hid in her hair. Somehow they ended up in her hair because they like dark places and the hair spray made this shield like *Gardol* on the toothpaste commercial where the decay can't get through the toothpaste. And the black widow spiders got trapped within her hairdo in this wall of hair spray and got panicked and couldn't get out and ate their way through her skull. Bit her in the skull to get out and that's how she died. (*Bert and Joanne neck.*)

DONNY. Bert?

MARGIE. Can I have a bite of that bran muffin?

DONNY. Bert? Is your mother at work?

JOANNE. Bran is supposed to be the secret of life.

BERT. You feel like getting another wrist watch?

MARGIE. How'd that woman do her hair? (*Bert and Donny get up and go. Joanne begins demonstrating. The lights come down on the luncheonette . . . a fanfare of music. Lights up on Rosalie, L., by her piano. She prepares herself for the next scene, putting on a red kimono.*)

ROSALIE. Flashback. Eighteen months ago. I was still among the living. How my sister and nephew came to New York in the first place. (*Lights up on Rosalie's apartment. Rosalie moves into the scene. The apartment contains a sink, a table, a chair, a day bed strewn with clothes, a vanity. Rosalie's waking up and putting on makeup and drinking coffee and looking in the mirror. Betty looks different than we have seen before. Two years ago, she was very plain. Very nervous.*)

BETTY. Rosalie, you got to come home. You're growing up not knowing your family. Your nephew. Our mother. (*Bert shyly looks out from under his mother's arm.*)

ROSALIE. Hiya, kid. Want a snort?

BETTY. Tell her, Bert.

BERT. Bangor, Maine is about the greatest place I know. It's not like the old days when nothing was there. Bangor, Maine is the home of one of the world's busiest airports. (*Bert holds out a pennant marked "Bangor."*)

ROSALIE. He's great.

BERT. Bangor, Maine is the center of the chartered jet service that takes Americans to all parts of the globe on budget flights.

ROSALIE. You done good, Betty.

BETTY. Rosalie, Bangor is so interesting. You meet people from all over the world who are laying over. Lots of times they're fogged in and you get to hear about their travels and I sell souvenirs and there's an opening in the cocktail lounge. You could sing. You'd meet such interesting people. I pray for snow. I pray for fog. All the things that used to make life so dismal in Bangor are now the exact things that make it so interesting.

ROSALIE. Honeybunch, you're hearing about the world. But hearing about don't put no notches on anyone's pistol. I'm doing. Bert, would you go out onto Christopher Street to the Li-Lac Chocolate store and request about a pound of kisses? (*She gives Bert money. Bert goes.*)

BETTY. Bert, you be careful. Is it safe out there?

ROSALIE. Honeybunch, I get this call last week, would I be interested appearing in a film. Sure, why not.

BETTY. He's never been to a city before.

ROSALIE. I report to a motel on Forty Second Street and Eleventh Avenue. Way west. Take elevator to the sixth floor. Knock. Go in. Flood lights. A camera. Workmen setting up. The real thing! A man said, "You the girl?" Get your duds off. Sink into the feathers and go to it. Holy shit, they're loading the cameras and I'm naked and nobody's really paying attention. They say, "You all set?" Sure, why not. Lights. Camera. Action. And a door I thought was a closet opens up and it's from another room and a gorilla leaps out with a slit in his suit and this enormous erection and the gorilla jumps on me. Honeybunch, there's no surprises like that in Maine. And we're going at it and I can't believe it and after about five minooties, the director yells "Cut!" and the gorilla rolls off me, takes off his gorilla head and it's Harry Reems from *Deep Throat* and *The Devil in Miss Jones*. What an honor to meet you, sir, I said. Christ! Go back to Bangor, Maine! Honey, you should

20

move in with me. Get yourself unsaddled from Momma and that house and airports.

BETTY. It's our family.

ROSALIE. Honeybaby, start your own family. I started my own family. I've got a family motto. *She Travels Fastest Who Travels Alone.* I live here on Christopher Street. A lovely building. Lovely neighbors. Leave you alone. Nobody knows me. I don't know anybody. I'm flying high. I'm working for a travel agency. *Dawn's Promising Star Travel Agency.* Founder and sponsor of Honeymoon Holidays. No charter jets for me. When I travel, which shall be soon, I'll be traveling First Class not out of Bangor, but right out of old JFK. Wait till you meet my boss, Raulito. Take it back. Erase those tapes. You'll never meet him. I'd show you my life, you'd get so jealous, you'd want to move right in and take me over. You can't have me. You can have yourself but you can't have me. Ditch the kid. He comes from a whole other rotten period of your life. Erase those tapes. Get rid of him. I got a pull-out sofa. Move in. We can have some laughs.

BETTY. I've got lots of laughs in Bangor. When it isn't raining, it's snowing. I meet boys at the airport, but they end up taking planes. Momma sits by the TV singing *Rosalie My Darling.* Aside from that everything's okay.

ROSALIE. Listen, send the kid back. There's an extra key.

BETTY. Momma sent me down here to bring you back.

ROSALIE. You just wire a little wire to Momma. Hey, Momma, send me a change of address card. I get lonely, Honeybunch. We could have some laughs. I'm proud of my life and I'd like to show it off to you. We're young. (*Bert enters with a box of chocolates.*) Hiya, kid. We were just talking about you.

BERT. Kisses! (*The lights go out on Bert and Betty in Rosalie's apartment. Rosalie whips off her bathrobe and steps in time to the very jazzy piano music. Behind the stage is bare, black. A cyclist wearing a mask, goggles, helmet, shorts, appears u. holding a bicycle over his head. As Rosalie speaks to us, he advances slowly, threateningly, towards her.*)

ROSALIE. So I walk out on Christopher, cut down on Bleecker to walk to work and I'm just jazzing along Hudson Street, and you know where that Ristorante Rigoletto is that the papers gave eighteen tureens to and they got limousines parked out front and I happen to know the chef sprays fresh herbs on the canned Boyardee, but, what the hell, it's over-priced, out of the way, they treat you like shit, and Uptown loves it. Well, I'm being so specific because it's just at that very location that a ten-speed yellow Raleigh bike bears down on me. I apparently splattered up against the window of the Ristorante Rigoletto like a pizza that suddenly appeared on the menu. My last thoughts were of Betty moving down to New York. I won her. Revenge on our Momma. I was feeling very happy. (*The sound of a crash. Rosalie shrugs her shoulders and goes into the dark. The masked man glares at us never lowering his bicycle.*)

MASKED MAN. I don't give a shit if she's dead! Who's gonna fix my bike? The chain is off my bike! Who's gonna pay for that? Give me the bag. She owes me money. Life belongs to the living. I don't give a shit if she just died. She should've looked. I am traveling. I am moving. Who's gonna pay for my bike? Chocolate? That's all she's got in the fucking bag? Chocolate kisses? How am I supposed to fix my bike with chocolate kisses? She deserves to die. (*He walks off into black. Lights up on Rosalie who sits by the piano and sings:*)

ROSALIE. (*Sings.*)
>Was that Mister Right?*
>If it was, I'll let it pass.
>The right Mister Right
>That funky looking skunk put me kerplunk on my ass
>I thought Mister right
>Would have a little more couth.
>He'd come on a white charger
>Say Hi-de-hi to my charm
>And Vo-de-oh to my youth

(*The bright jazz tune plays.*) So Betty Yearn newly arrived from Bangor, Maine stays in New York to settle my estate along with my hash. She moves into my apartment, she takes over my job. I'm not even cool in the grave yet, and she's got my job. She moves into my life. Betty Yearns's first day 18 months ago in the Dawn's Promising Star Travel Agency. A division of Honeymoon Holidays. (*The jazz music turns Latin. Lights up on the travel agency: A desk. A telephone. Lots of telephone books. A cassette recorder that contains tapes of cheering and applause. Betty is dressed in a pretty outfit for her first day at work. And if she can wear pants and look*

---

* Music for this song appears at end of playbook.

pretty, Raulito can wear what appears to be—is it? —a gold lamé evening gown over his business suit, and still look mucho macho. Raulito is very handsome like a 1940's Latin leading man with a pompadour and diamond rings. He carries an armful of Sunday's papers. He is sexually very threatening and makes Betty even more fearful than she generally is.)

RAULITO. You take the *Daily News*. You take the Sunday *Times*. Not the financial section. Not the sports section.

BETTY. There's so many sections.

RAULITO. The engagement section.

BETTY. The society page.

RAULITO. You look up the name of the father, the man who is paying for the wedding.

BETTY. Mr. and Mrs. Bernard Culkin of Corona and Point Lookout announce the engagement of their daughter, Lillibet—

RAULITO. Stop right there. You look in the phone book. Not the Manhattan phone book.

BETTY. So I look up Corona in . . . there are so many phone books. I've only been here a few days.

RAULITO. Corona is in Queens.

BETTY. Culkin. BBBBBB Bernard.

RAULITO. Don't *show* it to me. Copy the phone number down on the pad.

BETTY. I swear to you, I'm generally very good at writing numbers.

RAULITO. Check the bride-to-be's name.

BETTY. Lillibet.

RAULITO. See what Lillibet does? Where Lillibet is employed.

BETTY. Educated at St. John's University.

RAULITO. Your sister was like streaks of lightning here.

BETTY. Is employed as a researcher at Mutual Life.

RAULITO. So she should be home at 5:30. Mark down to call her at?

BETTY. 5:45?

RAULITO. 5:31!

BETTY. Nice to have a few minutes to get your coat off.

RAULITO. Your late and more and more lamented sister would have that phone ringing off the hook the instant Lillibet Culkin Corona Queens stuck her key in the door.

BETTY. Fine.

23

RAULITO. If I may be so bold, petals on a pool drifting, you want a travel brochure back to Bangor?

BETTY. No! I feel my sister wanted me to have this job.

RAULITO. No hard feelings. We can be friends. If I'm ever in Bangor, God forbid. I'll look you up. Is the job too hard for you?

BETTY. I can do it.

RAULITO. Then, honey through the comb sifting, you must be prepared to play Follow the Leader. Miss Lisa Staminelli to wed law student. Bayside, Queens. Father Frank Staminelli. Presented to society the Gotham Ball. You have the Queens phone book. Zut zut zut zut *zutt* you have the number. You dial it. (*He accomplishes this task in a brilliant quick stroke.*) This is where my Rosalie was brilliant. (*Into phone.*) Miss Lisa Staminelli. Is she there? Is this she? This is she? The noted debutante? I am talking to her. Ohhhhh, Miss Staminelli, this is *Bride's Magazine* calling. Of course I'm breathless. Are you sitting down? Miss Staminelli, you've won our lottery. An all-expense paid honeymoon for two to Paradise Cove. Two weeks!

BETTY. Two weeks?

RAULITO. Yes! For you and Mr. Right— (*Checks paper.*) Bruce Mandrake. How did I know? Darling, we here at *Bride's Magazine* know *tout!* If we didn't know who was getting married, we wouldn't know if the world would keep spinning. We need families and families are love and love pulled your number out of the lottery. Fate wanted you and your new husband, Mr. Mandrake—is he the magician? —to have this honeymoon. Do you think it's possible, God, we know you're so busy. Would it be possible for you and *Senor* Right to stop down to our office to pick up your honeymoon? Fourteenth Street. 618 West. Ninth floor. The Honeymoon Holidays Building. Could you and Bruce toddle on down here any night after work, say seven? We could finalize arrangements for the honeymoon? Some forms to sign. (*Music becomes a tango.*) Then you could have a lovely evening in the Village. Greenwich Village. Chianti. Pasta. Discuss your future. Discuss your honeymoon. It's all luck and love is luck and you're the luckiest girl in the world, Lisa. The past shows us the mistakes we made. The future's the place where we won't make them again. Dreams are the fuel for reality. A new family is coming into the world! Oh God! Grab the now! The now is all quicksilver and mercury. The now is diamonds. Can I make an appointment for you? (*Music stops.*) Lucky you! I could squeeze you in tomorrow at seven ten. Oh, Lisa, you've made all of us so happy at *Bride's Magazine*. (*Puts on cassette of cheering.*) See you tomorrow. (*Hangs up.*) You're the bait, baby. You lure them in here. *You* decorate the hook. *I* make the sale.

BETTY. Everybody falls for it?

RAULITO. Sometimes a black eye. Every now and then a death threat. But, Sweetness and Light, if I can make one sale a week, that is two trips to the Caribbean. I can make out all right. Besides what is living without a little danger?

BETTY. Do they ever call *Bride's Magazine*?

RAULITO. Only the smart ones and they're not exactly our clientele.

BETTY. Could we be sued?

RAULITO. By who?

BETTY. *Bride's Magazine*.

RAULITO. For what?

BETTY. I don't want to go to jail. My life is beginning. I don't want to be arrested.

RAULITO. Hey, hey, hey. Evidence obtained by wire tap is illegal. Can't be introduced into court. What planet you from anyway, baby?

BETTY. What borough is the moon in?

RAULITO. The moon is the fifty-first state. Hawaii. Alaska. The moon. Did you see the moon last night? Like a little Turkish flag waving in the sky? I saluted.

BETTY. Why do you dress that way?

RAULITO. That is exactly what your sister Rosalie said to me the first time we met. We would curl up on her pull-out sleep sofa, now *your* pull-out sleep sofa and I would tell her my dream to one night turn on the TV and hear the Late Show say "And tonight our guest is ME!" (*He puts on his cassette of cheering.*) Thank you Johnny. I'm from Cuba. We lived on the other side of the island. From Havana. (*The piano plays Latin style. Raulito sits beside the desk as if he were the guest on the "Tonight Show" and Betty were the host.*) Poor. You never saw such poor. We were so poor *that*. You know those jokes? He was so fat *that*. She was so dumb *that*. Well, we were so *poor* that. When I was wearing rags, I was running around naked. This part of Cuba that we called the country, I think any normal thinking person would call it the jungle. Occasionally, a magazine would appear in our village and I'd see the pictures of evening gowns and spangles and barettes

25

in the hair and these high heels. I didn't know till later that was what women wore. I thought that was rich people. I thought if you were rich and lived in the city or lived in America that was what the average American family hung around in. The Revolution came. I saw Che Guevara this close. We left Cuba. We got to Florida. Where I found out that those uniforms with diamonds and lace did not belong to the typical American man. But a few years ago, I was shopping in the Salvation Army for a winter coat and I came upon this real Rita Hayworth special. A beautiful 1940's evening gown for twenty five cents. I bought it. Why not. The dreams we have as kids they're the dreams we never get over. I put it on over my suit. I feel rich. I feel successful. (*Raulito begins to spin so the dress flares out. He advances seductively on Betty, now waving his dress like a matador's cape in front of her. Betty is terrified. Raulito shows no mercy.*) I feel I can get out of the jungle and get to America and twirl and twirl. Feeling good outside I start to feel good inside. I start Honeymoon Holidays. I want to start a family. I want to start a life. Betty, your sister went with me. Your sister would let me dance with her first. Then she would let me sleep with her after and dreams would come out of our heads like little Turkish moons. We would salute. Betty?

BETTY. (*Getting back to work.*) It's about 5:30. I'd better call Lillibet.

RAULITO. You like the name Lillibet?

BETTY. It's a name. People have names. I take the Queens phone book.

RAULITO. Do you know what Queen Elizabeth's secret name is? If you were in her royal family what you would call her?

BETTY. Elizabeth. They'd call her Elizabeth. They'd call her Queen Elizabeth. Elizabeth is short for Queen Elizabeth.

RAULITO. They'd call her Lillibet.

BETTY. I thought I was safe when I came in here, when I met you at my sister's funeral I thought this guy's a weirdo but I'll be safe.

RAULITO. Lillibet is the Queen's secret name. What Prince Philip calls her when they're alone. I read that in *People's* magazine. Alone must mean also in the royal bed. Prince Philip calls over to her: Lillibet? He turns on the royal radio station. A little English Latin music comes on the royal radio. I should call you Lillibet. Tell me your story? Unfold yourself to me?

BETTY. I'm Betty. Betty's short for Elizabeth. I'm a Betty. That's all I am. I have no story. I'm no guest on any talk show. No story. I am

26

a middle aged woman. I'm a young girl. I'm regular. Quiet. Normal. Human person. (*She is shaking violently. She puts on the cheering on the cassette. She dials telephone.*) Is Miss Lillibet Culkin there? Hi! This is *Bride's Magazine* calling. The lottery of love twirled and stopped at . . . oh? The wedding is off? The groom is dead? Head injuries. Attacked by a monkey wrench. Greenwich Village. Beaten brutally. Watch stolen. I don't care. Don't tell me your troubles. You won a honeymoon. That's all I want to tell you. That's all. (*Hangs up.*) Lillibet Culkin. Corona, Queens. I don't want the job. I can't handle the job. I'm not my sister. I am not Rosalie. I can't do her job. I'm not Lillibet. I'm not Queen Elizabeth. I'm nobody. I'm me. I can't do the job. I don't want the job. (*Raulito has picked her up. He tangos her away into the dark. Rosalie appears by piano. She sings while the travel agency is being replaced by the apartment.*)

ROSALIE.

Frightened of you*
All of these years
Never secure
In your embrace
Sleep through the night
Dream that I'm dead
Feeling your weight
There in the bed
One little bag
Never unpacked
Hidden away
In case
I get the nerve
One day to leave
Finally that fact
To face
What's getting me through my life?
What's my excuse inside?
What's keeping me in my life?
The molehill of lust or the mountain of pride?
Forgive me, my dear
A slip of the tongue
Forget what I said

* Music for this song appears at end of playbook.

Erase
I meant to say
My life is brightened by you
The darkness whitened by you
Each moment heightened by you
My life enlightened by you
But not I'm frightened of you
Forgive me
I'm sorry
Don't hit me
I love you

A year and a half later. Eighteen count'em eighteen months. My sister has moved into my life. It's like two days before the boy's murder. (*Lights* u. *on Betty and Raulito necking, passionately. He has gathered his evening gown up under the trench coat he now wears. Betty is quite snappily dressed and a lot more sure of herself in the last months since we've seen her. The music is ominous. Rosalie goes into black. Raulito kisses Betty one time more and he goes into dark. The lights come up on the apartment. Bert sits on a red bean bag winding watches. He tenses. Betty straightens herself. She comes in the room. Begins to take off her dress and put on a robe.*)

BETTY. I bought this new dress today. You like it? (*Takes another dress out of a paper bag.*) Or do you like this one? What do you think moving maybe to Miami? I got a chance finally after eighteen months at Raulito's. A free trip for two. National Airlines. There's a lot of cities we could fly to. L.A. Round trip ticket but, we could just stay. Stop winding all those watches. I never saw anyone for finding so many watches. Find 'em and wind 'em. That's your name. The watch monster. That's what I gave birth to. Can't you say anything? Jesus. Who'd've thought you'd grow up to be your father. To have to live through all that again. Can't you say anything.

BERT. How's Honeymoon Holidays?

BETTY. Raulito called me a professional today. He gave me a gold star. (*Picks up phone.*) Miss Mary Louise Nicholson? The lottery of love twirled and twirled and stopped at your number. It don't hurt to start a marriage with a good honeymoon. (*She slams phone down.*)

BERT. Did you and Daddy have a good honeymoon?

BETTY. If I had a good honeymoon, you think I'd be working at Honeymoon Holidays?

BERT. You going to marry Raulito?

BETTY. Raulito already has a wife and about nineteen children. He gave me this butterfly pin. It was his grandmother's. (*She bends it.*) Now you bend it. I don't want anybody doing nice for me. (*Bert bends the pin. Betty throws the pin away.*) I don't want anybody giving me presents. I don't want to be reminded what I missed out on. We should've had a family. We could've had a family. A regular dynasty. I had a family. I should've passed one on to you. If we'd had a family, we'd go to the movies and eat at McDonald's and take summer trips to Maine to see your grandmother and see free Shakespeare in the park and take long rides on the subway to the Bronx Zoo and the Brooklyn Botanicals. If we had a family, things'd be a lot different around here.

BERT. Why can't we do all those things now? They're all free.

BETTY. Because they're things families do together. Because they remind me how I screwed up my life. If we don't do nothing, I don't get reminded. But I don't want to turn you against your father. I want you to love your father. Your father was a god. Your father was the handsomest man I ever saw. Your father had a body you could see through his clothes. Your father had shoulders out to here and a waist you could clasp your thumb and index finger around. A brain of a fucking wizard. He could remember telephone numbers. Addresses. He could remember lottery numbers and the social security numbers of people he met a hundred years ago. Serial numbers of guys he was in the Army with. He was kind of creepy when you come to think of it.

BERT. He sounds great.

BETTY. We bumped into an old Army buddy and your father said "I remember you. 19769982." The guy says "Hey, why'd you remember my serial number?" Your father says "Hold on. I haven't been thinking about you all these years. I just happen to have that kind of memory."

BERT. So why's he forgot where we live?

BETTY. A blind spot. He forgot you. He forgot me. For a guy with a memory. What I think is living on Christopher Street. Ever since the Catholic Church said St. Christopher doesn't exist, maybe he thinks Christopher Street doesn't exist either.

BERT. But you left him.

BETTY. I didn't mind him, well, I did, him putting my head down the toilet and flushing it. But you. When he put your head down the toilet and flushed it, I said that's it. And I told him to leave.

BERT. I have dreams sometimes of water rushing by me.

BETTY. That comes from your father putting your head down the toilet.

BERT. I think I'll join the Navy when I can. The submarine service.

BETTY. You been seeing too many Walt Disney movies. (*Joanne runs in breathless.*)

JOANNE. You know what my mother told me today? A lady in her office knew a lady who died and they couldn't find a reason why she died. She was healthy.

BETTY. I don't want to hear any more black widow spiders. You get me?

JOANNE. This isn't black widow spiders. This is the truth. This lady died and they traced all her steps and they found she had gone to Korvette's Department Store and on her dead body they found her wearing a beautiful Indian blouse with pieces of mirror sewn in it.

BETTY. Sounds pretty. Korvette's?

JOANNE. And they traced all her steps and went to Korvette's and opened the drawer where the Indian blouses came from and they reached in and the detective pulled back his hand because it almost got bit by a cobra. Which is what happened to the lady. These blouses had come in from India. And cobra eggs had got woven in beneath the mirrors while the blouses were being made and the cobra eggs hatched from the heat of being mailed over here and the lady reached her hand in the drawer and got bitten and died. (*Betty serves Bert dinner. Bert eats.*)

BETTY. Where is this woman? How come you always have these friends who are getting bit by black widow spiders? Bit by cobras.

BERT. It was her mother's friend.

BETTY. I don't believe her mother.

BERT. Then you don't believe me. Are you calling me a liar.

BETTY. I don't want you hanging around together. I don't want any more stories about black widow spiders and black widow cobras. I'm up to here with it. (*Joanne runs out.*) And you be careful with her. I don't want any fourteen year old fathers living in my house. I'm not ready to be a grandmother yet.

BERT. You old hag. You old crone. I know how old you are. You're thirty six and you're gonna die soon and I'm fourteen and I'm going to live forever. I hate you. You're going to die. You know what I want for Christmas? You in a coffin under a Christmas tree. Why did Aunt Rosalie have to die? Why couldn't you be the one that bicycle hit. Maybe that guy is around right now speeding down streets looking for you.

BETTY. You know why you can't hurt me? Cause I have X-ray eyes and I can see right into your heart.

BERT. Bullshit.

BETTY. Remember that old man with the push cart in Bangor who called out *OLD CLOTHES?* You used to follow him for hours. What did you do with that filthy old man? *Old Clothes.* I place my X-ray eyes over you and I see deep in you *Old Clothes. Old Clothes. Old Clothes.*

BERT. Don't say that.

BETTY. Old clothes. Old rags. Old rats. X-ray eyes.

BERT. Don't say that! Don't say that!

BETTY. Don't have to say it. I feel it. I'm being very quiet and saying to myself over and over. (*Wordless:*) Old clothes. (*Bert hits her. She hits him back.*)

BERT. Shut up! Shut up!

BETTY. I'm not saying anything. (*Wordless:*) Old clothes.

BERT. It's what you're thinking. Can't think that. Stop! Stop!

BETTY. I love thinking. I can think anything I want.

BERT. I've killed people.

BETTY. Don't make me laugh.

BERT. I haven't killed them. Donny's killed them.

BETTY. There you are. You couldn't hurt a fly. I do mean that as a compliment. I mean that as a truth. You could not wound a mosquito. If David and Goliath had a fight, Goliath would reach down and squeeze your head like a seedless grape.

BERT. I lure them up here while you're away and Donny and I kill them. Hit them on the head with the monkey. Take their watches. Roll them out in the hall. They don't dare call the cops on us. I can so hurt a fly.

BETTY. (*Slaps him.*) Lure? Where'd you learn a word like lure?

BERT. I know a lot of words.

BETTY. There's a whole series of murders going around.

BERT. Maybe that's me.

BETTY. Decapitations.

BERT. What's that?

BETTY. Down at all these rough bars down by the river, Raulito told me at work they find people with heads chopped off. The police don't bother to check them out. It's not worth the trouble. You're not part of those murders, are you? I told you to stay away from those docks, you little faggot.

BERT. What's decap—decap—

BETTY. Chop their heads off!

BERT. I didn't do that! I swear! I'm just into watches. Money. The monkey wrench. I don't think any of them ever died. I swear. (*A man appears at the door. A large man, carefully dressed in a white linen suit, Panama hat and black string tie. He carries flowers.*)

BETTY. Yes?

MAN. Betty? Betty Mandible?

BETTY. I was.

BERT. Are you the police?

MAN. You got married.

BETTY. Oh yes. My husband here and I are very happy. Some people say he's too young. I say why not?

MAN. Hello, Betty.

BERT. My mother says go away. She doesn't know you. Ma? Is this guy bothering you?

BETTY. I know who you are.

MAN. I was hoping you would.

BETTY. Narragansett. Summer of—

MAN. Nineteen years ago. I'm Durwood Peach.

BETTY. Durwood Peach. The Good Humor Man. Pushing that white ice cream truck.

DURWOOD. Name like a flavor ice cream. The special may be blueberry ripple but I'm pushing the peach.

BETTY. You were from North—

DURWOOD. South.

BETTY. Carolina. You came up to Bangor, to visit your aunt.

DURWOOD. Can I sit down for a minute? Excuse me for not being on my toes more. Oh, I have been driving. I drove from South Carolina straight up to Bangor, Maine and looked up your name in the phone book. Your mother answered. She told me your swell sister had passed on. She told me you were here. You were the one I wanted. I got back in my car and drove from Maine nonstop here to Christopher Street. So this is Greenwich Village. Sure is lively. Mexican restaurant and a Chinese restaurant and an Indian restaurant all one block. A lot of variety, your mother didn't mention you had a little boy. Is he yours?

BERT. I'm hers.

BETTY. Why are you here?

DURWOOD. See. Now I should said that soon as I arrived. I never forgot you nineteen years ago and even though we never talked much and you had other boy friends and you and me never went out, I have recently realized you are the only girl I ever loved, ever will love. My doctor gave me a note saying all this was true.

BETTY. Doctor?

DURWOOD. I been in a hospital and I got out and I been going to a doctor and you appeared to me like a holy movie when the Blessed Virgin appears and tells the holy children what to do. You appeared in my analysis. Here's the note.

BETTY. Thank you. (*Takes the note.*)

DURWOOD. Now my knees are shaking. I'm gonna faint.

BERT. Should I call the police?

DURWOOD. No! I'm all right. It's all the driving from South Carolina to Bangor, Maine back to New York. Betty. I love you. I'll always love you. I've never loved anyone else. I've told my wife. She understands. She's written a note to you giving me up to you.

BETTY. (*Reads.*) "Dear Betty. I surrender all rights to Durwood heartbroken and bereft as that leaves me."

DURWOOD. My grandfather, the only surviving member of my natural family, the head of the clan, welcomes you in to the family. I'm rich, Betty. I've got a farm and I lease it out to a racetrack and I make lots of money. Here's a thousand dollars in single new bills as a sign of faith. You remember me. I didn't have to introduce myself. I thought I'd have to introduce myself. That's a good sign. You remember me.

BERT. You want me to get my monkey? Bang him down on his head? I can get Donny down here.

BETTY. I never even kissed you.

DURWOOD. To pursue the unattainable. My doctor says that's my problem.

BETTY. The unattainable I'm afraid I must remain.

DURWOOD. No, you won't. I won't lie to you. I have been sick. And to be cured, I must once in my life obtain the unobtainable or I will die. I'm staying at the Dixie Hotel on West Forty Second Street. I'll return there now and leave this one thousand dollars to show my good faith. I'll leave these photos of my farm and all that you'll be mistress of. A mountain. A river. Caves that are closed to the public. I'll give you time to peruse my offer and would like to ask your permission to call tomorrow night after which time perhaps we could leave immediately. You cannot escape from me or the power of my mind. We will begin a family. I'll be cured. We'll be happy. All these years. I'll be back tomorrow evening at six P.M. with my bags packed. I'll make a reservation at the Mexican restaurant for two.

BERT. For three.

DURWOOD. For two. Betty. You and me.

BETTY. I don't think you need reservations at Taco Trolley.

DURWOOD. Until tomorrow, Betty. Your mother's angry at you. She said she sent you down here to bring your sister back and you never returned. She said she had messages for you. She said get in touch. If I can bring you together, you and your mother, that'll be doing good. My doctor will be so happy. He said if you really want her, you'll find her. I didn't have to call. You were home. One of the largest cities in the world. You were here. Now I'm here. I'll be back tomorrow. The special is blueberry. But I'm pushing the peach. (*Durwood goes. Bert has been counting the money Durwood left behind.*)

BETTY. I got to sit down.

BERT. You think it's counterfeit? You bend the face in half on two bills and if theyl fit together, the two faces into one face, that proves it's not counterfeit.

BETTY. I remember him.

BERT. You must've been the prettiest girl around that summer.

BETTY. I was pretty. But not this pretty. Do you think he's telling the truth. South Carolina? Should I go? Maybe he does have money. Get us out of here. Who cares if he's a nut. It's amazing how a little tomorrow can make up for a whole lot of yesterday.

It sounds like one of those uplift songs in a musical comedy.
(Sings:) "It's amazing how a little tomorrow."
BERT. (Sings.) "Makes up for a whole lot of yesterday."
BETTY. "It's amazing how a little tomorrow." Do you have a
joint? A jay? Don't do lies to me. I found them in the Saltine box
the last time.
BERT. This time I hid the dope in the one place you'd never look.
BETTY. Stop making with the funnies . . . I want to keep this
moment. I feel it going away all ready and I'm hanging on to it.
Don't go away, magic moment. I'll be right there.
BERT. The one place you'd never look.
BETTY. I give up.
BERT. The broom closet.
BETTY. You're right. The one place I'd never look. I like giant
dustballs. It gives me a flavor of the Old West. (They sit on the
day-bed and light up. The lights dim slightly on them as they
smoke. Rosalie and her piano appear in light at L. Rosalie sings it
like one of those rousing up-lift songs in a musical comedy.)
ROSALIE.
ITS AMAZING HOW A LITTLE TOMORROW*
    It's amazing how a little tomorrow
    Can make up for a whole lot of yesterday
    It's amazing how a little tomorrow
    Can make up for a whole lot of yesterday
    Yesterday was dreary
    Clocks kept on crawling
    Now the future's cheery
    How thrilling, how enthralling
    It's amazing how a little tomorrow
    Can recompense an awful lot of sorrow
    So get yourself a little tomorrow
    And wake up from those awful yesterdays.
    It's amazing how a little tomorrow
    Can recompense an awful lot of sorrow
    So get yourself a little tomorrow
    And wake up those awful yesterdays.
    Shake up all those bore-filled yesterdays.
    Make up those unlawful yesterdays.
(She dances back to the piano. They bow and go into darkness.

* Music for this song appears at end of playbook.

Lights up on Betty and Bert. Bert and Betty sit on the day-bed.)
BETTY. The first time I ever smoked pot, I was in a bar in Rhode Island with my girl friend.
BERT. (*Is bombed by the joint.*) The summer you met Durwood?
BETTY. No, after. This guy asked us if we wanted to smoke reefers and my girl friend said "Only if you promise we'll turn into sex crazed nymphomanics who won't be held responsible for any of their activities." (*A man appears* u. *in light, dressed like a beatnik.*) And the man said:
MAN. (*Striking a match.*) Results guaranteed.
BETTY. And off we went. He had a car.
MAN. (*Lighting cigarette.*) Get in.
BETTY. What's that black rag?
MAN. I'm going to have to blindfold you girls seeing as how I am the Dope King of Providence, Rhode Island.
BETTY. Ooooo, I love an expert. Shut up, Betty. Just shut up.
DOPE KING. Lookit, you little twats, if you ever got caught, you couldn't reveal where I'd taken you. You couldn't betray me, but then I couldn't have you betray yourselves with the knowledge you knew where the dope headquarters of Providence, Rhode Island was. I'm doing this for you, you little twats.
BETTY. We drove, the three of us, my girl friend, him, me. We giggled suicidally because maybe this man steering his car right then left then left then right would murder us and if he did we should remember where he took us. I had hear that directions given before death stay embroidered on your brain and the police can use that for a clue. I didn't care if we were murdered. My life was beginning. There was a hit song that summer. We drove singing it. (*Betty sings in a clear, pure voice.*)

> Hey Stay a While*
> In the crook of my arms
> All you got to do is
> Look in my arms
> And you'll see Home Sweet Home
> I'll invest in a doormat
> Hey Home Sweet Home
> We'll test the mattress
> Our arms are sinuous
> All performances are continuous

* Music for this song appears at end of playbook.

Hey Stay a While
Feel the smile in my arms
And the smile's in my arms
All for you
Sit back/Relax
Cool brow/Tension slacks
Hey Stay a while
My arms are filled with
What the whole world lacks
Hey Stay a While

Mavis, because that was my girl friend's name, Mavis Brennan is squeezing my hand and I'm squeezing hers. Where are we? I smell bread. That Portuguese bakery. I think I know where we are.

DOPE KING. We're here.

BETTY. He led us out of the car. We held hands like mountain climbers. Doors open. Stairs climb.

MAN. Okay. Open your eyes.

BETTY. Three steps. One. Two. Three. Doors shut. It was the room I had lived in the year before when I was working in the shoe factory for the summer. I saw traces on the wall where I had written "Fuck You" in peanut butter the year before one night because here I was seventeen and my life still hadn't begun and I'm out supporting myself. I said "Is Miss Carter the landlady here? Is that the shoe factory over there?" I said "Boy, some dope king. Living in a seventeen dollar a week rooming house with breakfast thrown in on Saturday."

DOPE KING. Some breakfast. (*The lights go off on the Dope King.*)

BETTY. (*Watching where he went.*) We laughed and laughed.

BERT. That's nice. You go to a strange place and they take off your blindfolders and it's a place where you lived.

BETTY. That is precisely what I did not underline the not, did not like. I remember Miss Carter had said "What's that word in peanut butter on the wall." I said "Oh, you think that says Fuck? You dirty lady. That's a message in speedwriting. If You See Kay." "Kay was my girl friend," I said. "If you see Kay, remind us both to rd ths msj and gt a bttr jb." Memories within memories. I'm remembering what I remembered in my memory . . .

BERT. Where's Mavis?

BETTY. She died or something.

37

BERT. Mavis Brennan.

BETTY. Don't be such a busy body.

BERT. Mavis Brennan.

BETTY. What am I telling you stories about dope for. I should be telling you stories how I didn't take dope. I should be a father influence to you.

BERT. How did you die?

BETTY. Who died?

BERT. Mavis Brennan.

BETTY. Don't be so morbid. I didn't say she died.

BERT. You said she died.

BETTY. Or something.

BERT. What's the something?

BETTY. You lose touch. Touch gets lost.

BERT. Will I lose touch with you?

BETTY. You're my kid. You're me. You're the fruit of my loins or the fruit of my loom. Some joke Mavis and I used to make about phases in the Bible. Jesus came riding into town on his ass. We'd laugh. I wish sometimes you were a girl. I wish sometimes I had a friend. Mavis Brennan.

BERT. You can call me Mavis.

BETTY. Mavis, I'm in love with a boy named Bert.

BERT. Do you love him a lot?

BETTY. More than life itself.

BERT. Do you love life?

BETTY. More than Bert himself.

BERT. Do you love me?

BETTY. But Mavis, you're my best friend.

BERT. Can I rub your hair?

BETTY. (Sits at kitchen table.) Oh, yes, Mavis.

BERT. (Rubs her hair.) When I rub your hair, I can feel the oil from it under my fingernails. I sit in class and the teacher says "Get your fingers out of your nose." He says "You can always tell the Catholic kids from the Protestant kids." He says "The Catholic kids are always picking their nose and the Protestant kids are always biting their nails." He's bald and he says "Grass doesn't grow on busy streets."

BETTY. You tell him grass doesn't grow on rocks either. This feels so good . . . don't stop . . . Bert . . . Mavis . . .

38

BERT. (*Bert goes to sink, takes tray containing basin, pitcher, water and shampoo.*) I'm getting the basin.

BETTY. I washed my hair last night.

BERT. Let me wash it tonight? Please? Momma, we have a thousand dollars in bills of consecutive numbers. You are loved. You have decisions to make. Momma, let me clear your head. You always think better when I wash your hair. (*He pours hot water in her hair. She leans back. Her hair is undone. It streams out. Bert soaps it.*)

BETTY. Make it lather up. Push all the thoughts, the bad thoughts, push them out of my head.

BERT. Push 'em out. Push 'em out.

BETTY. (*Loving the shampoo.*) Wasn't he disgusting?

BERT. That man?

BETTY. (*Looking at the flowers he brought.*) Durwood Peach.

BERT. If you married him, you'd be Betty Peach.

BETTY. I'll give him his money back tomorrow.

BERT. Here comes the hot water!

BETTY. I'll keep half the money. A consideration fee. For considering his proposal.

BERT. Keep all of it. I don't want him around.

BETTY. No, I'll keep half the money in payment for a tormented night's sleep. For tossing and turning and wondering whether or not I should run away with an insane Good Humor man. Ex-Good Humor man.

BERT. Our flavor of the week: Betty Peach! Betty Peach on a stick! Here comes the shampoo. Make the bubbles come up. Work out all the bad thoughts.

BETTY. I went to visit Mavis in Memorial Hospital. She was dying of everything. They had cut off her breasts and she had lots of radiation treatment and her hair had gone. And I came to visit her. She was down to about sixty pounds and she wouldn't die. And I said, "Mavis, is there anything I can do for you?" And she said, "Yes, there is this new book: *The Sensuous Woman*. Bring it. Read it to me." And I went all that summer in Boston. Every day for visiting hours and read her from this dirty book on how to be sensuous and how to be attractive and how to have orgasms and how to . . . All summer she wouldn't die. All summer I read to her. I finished the book. Mavis said, "Begin it again." And I'd have to get very close to her to read to her because it was on the ward

39

and the other patients did not want to hear this dirty stuff. And her gums were black and her breath smelled like sulfur and her hair was gone and I'm reading her how to attract a man and she's smiling and hanging on. I never went back after one day. I couldn't go back. Fall was coming. I hated life. I hated Mavis. I hated. Rub the hair. Wash it out. More hot water. More bubbles. More soap. Get it all out of my head all the bad into a bubble and fly it away and pop it. Get it out. (*Betty has torn all the petals and leaves off the flowers.*)

BERT. (*Very moved, tender.*) The next time my biology teacher rubs his bald head and says "Grass doesn't grow on busy streets," I'll say, "Yeah and it doesn't grow on rocks either." I'll say that. I kiss your hair, Mama.

BETTY. And I kiss Mavis and you and Raulito and your father and the Dope King of Providence, Rhode Island and my sister Rosalie and life for bringing us a thousand dollars through the door and I kiss life and I kiss all the people I ever loved . . .

BERT. Me! Me! Most of all me! (*Bert pours water over her hair. The soap is washed out. Durwood appears in the room. He is breathless and excited.*)

DURWOOD. Is something wrong with me? I have you here and say goodnight like some goon. What am I being so polite about? I'm no goon. Good manners make you a goon. I'm trying to learn to listen to myself. Listen to what I want. Not what people tell me I should want. You must think I'm a goon. Only a goon would drive thousands of miles to find the only woman he ever loved, find her, then leave her and go back alone to a room in the Dixie Hotel by himself.

BETTY. (*Moving away from him.*) What did I do to make you feel all this?

DURWOOD. I remember riding by your house looking up at the porch, ringing the bells extra loud so you'd come down and buy ice cream from me. Your mother was sitting there rocking and your father reading a paper and you and your sister crouching on the green steps holding your skirts down around your ankles talking so hard to each other.

BETTY. They're all gone mostly.

BERT. You're gonna catch a cold. You got to dry the hair or the wet picks up dirt. Ma?

DURWOOD. You and your sister walked down the steps still

talking so hard you didn't even pay any attention to me and you bought vanilla and walked back up the stairs and sat down and kept on talking.

BETTY. What in God's name could we have been talking about?

DURWOOD. I said I want in. One day I'm going to be on that porch with that girl.

BETTY. Her leaving home? Some Ava Gardner movie?

DURWOOD. I realize now I wanted the girl and not the porch. (*Takes out snapshots.*) You got to come back with me. This house will be yours. All this land.

BERT. Look at all the fences. Everything is outlined.

DURWOOD. (*Tearing up photos.*) But if I had to choose between where I live and you, I'd rip up everything I own because the only landscape worth looking at is the landscape of the human body. I kiss your Blue Ridge Mountains of Virginia. I kiss your Missouri and Monongahela and Susquehanna and Shenandoah and Rio Grande. I kiss the confluence of all those rivers. I kiss your amber waves of grain. I kiss your spacious skies, your rocket's red glare, your land I love, your purple mountain'd majesty. But most of all I kiss your head. I kiss the place where we make our decisions. I kiss the place where we keep our resolves. The place where we do our dreams. I kiss the place behind the eyes where we store up secrets and knowledge to save us if we're caught in a corridor on a dark, wintry evening. And you, with your mouth, kiss my head because that's the place where I kept the pictures of you all these years. Come home with me to the hotel.

BETTY. I will come with you.

DURWOOD. (*Takes her aside.*) But you can't take the kid.

BERT. What is he saying?

DURWOOD. I don't want you having any children except what comes out of us.

BERT. What are you talking?

DURWOOD. A family's like a body. A perfect body. The man's the head. The woman's the heart. The children are the limbs. I don't want any limbs from any other bodies. No transplants allowed. You hear me? Only out of us.

BERT. What are you saying?

BETTY. (*Takes him aside, quiet.*) Let me go down there and check out the landscape. I'll send for you in a few days. I swear. (*Rosalie appears in the light, L.*)

41

ROSALIE. So they went to South Carolina. The two of them. They left the boy home. (*Captain Holahan appears in light,* R.) HOLAHAN. So she claims. So she claims. The fact remains the kid is dead. (*Betty holds out the money. Bert takes it. Black out.*)

ACT ONE CURTAIN

ACT TWO

Bert comes D. *and sings in a clear voice:*

BERT.
> I used to believe*
> When I was young
> I understood
> Every note that was sung.
> Voices of sparrows
> Voices of blue jays
> Voices of robins
> Voices of Eagles.
>
> When I was young
> I used to pretend
> Through all of my life
> I'd have a friend
> We'd climb the mountains
> We'd cross the deserts
> We'd sail the oceans
> We'd solve the mysteries.
>
> When I was young
> I used to believe
> In some other life
> I was an Inca
> Maybe a Druid
> More like Egyptian
> Pyramid builder
> Leader of millions.
>
> I used to believe
> When I was young
> I understood
> Every note that was sung . . .
>
> Voices of Eagles . . .

* Music for this song appears at end of playbook.

43

HOLAHAN. We had trouble tracking you down. You left town. Everybody thought you had taken the boy with you.

BETTY. I went away for a few days. He's a big kid. He's supposed to be able to take care of himself. Boy scouts go off. Survivor camps where they go off, kids, for three months, four, in mountains. Kids go in forests for weeks and months and they come out men and parents are applauded.

HOLAHAN. Bleecker Street ain't exactly survival camp.

BETTY. He was supposed to stay with people in the building were supposed to look after him.

HOLAHAN. A fourteen year old kid? Where's your head, lady?

BETTY. Here. This whole area above the neck. I just didn't desert him. I left him with money. I left him with a thousand dollars.

HOLAHAN. You left your kid with a thousand dollars?

BETTY. My friend that I traveled with gave it to him. To me. I gave it to Bert.

HOLAHAN. Even with inflation, a thousand's a lot of money.

BETTY. What I'm saying to you is find the person stole the thousand dollars, you'll find who murdered Bert. Said it. I said murdered Bert. I promised myself everything would be all right if I never mentioned the word murdered. If I just never said the word, I'd be all right. If I never said the word, the person who—did it—

HOLAHAN. The murderer—

BETTY. Would be found.

HOLAHAN. Stop running away from the fact!

BETTY. I am not running away from the fact—

HOLAHAN. Of the murder—

BETTY. I just promised myself I wouldn't name the fact. Not ever. You made me say the word.

HOLAHAN. Can I make you say another word you're avoiding?

BETTY. Confess? Mister, I can say the word confess all that I want because saying the word confess is like saying the word desk. Chair. Necktie. Dirt. Room. You. I have nothing to confess.

HOLAHAN. Where is this millionaire now?

BETTY. It was only a thousand.

HOLAHAN. This thousandaire. Where is he right now?

BETTY. South Carolina.

HOLAHAN. That's where you went?

44

BETTY. Solomon Ferry. The Peach family. Durwood. His father's name. He was a junior. (*Lights down on him as Holahan dials the phone. Rosalie appears in light, R. She drags a chair. She sits in it.*)
ROSALIE. Scene. In which Betty wishes her sister was still alive so she could tell her what happened. (*Betty sits against Rosalie's knees. Rosalie listens with a compassion and intensity she'd never have out of a fantasy.*)
BETTY. We got down to South Carolina two days after what a night at the Olde Dixie Hotel. Durwood wasn't kidding all right. We came down this alley of trees and he says "Close your eyes and now turn 'em on." He had this farm with white fences. I never saw so many white fences. I'm not even talking about what went on inside the white fences. I'm a country girl. No stranger to green. The horses and cattle. I never saw such fences. And roads. White painted rocks lining the roads pointing the way where you go up to the big house. I said "Boy, old girl, you hit pay dirt this time." "Boy, old girl," I said, "you have been on adventures in your short life time, but this is the key adventure. They're going to be doing TV spinoffs and shooting sequels to this part of your life. You are going to be a Southern lady." We stop in front of the white farm house and this youngish lady soon destined to be the ex-wife who wrote me the note struts out of the farm house followed by these two old people you just want to hug with a real nice parents' look followed by golden dogs the color gold of cough drops that rescue you in the middle of the night. Durwood gets out of the car and I let him walk around the car to let me out. And these people instead lead him in the house instead of letting him open my side of the door. The woman who would soon be Durwood's ex-wife came back out and said "Are you the girl from Maine?" I said "Yes, I was." She said "You're very kind to bring Durwood back to us. Here's money." I got out of the car. I said "I'm going to live here." The old people said "Thank you for bringing our boy back to us. Here's money. He had to get you out of his system. We let him go to you. The doctors said let him go. It was the only way." I said "Hey, this is going to be my house." "Well, one thing, Durwood isn't crazy about," they said, "is you. You sure are a pretty girl. He's been talking years about you. But it's time he goes back in for a rest. There's a bus leaving two oh five from Crossroads Corner going to Wheeling, West Virginia direct and you can make connections there back to Maine." I said "New York. I live in New

45

York now." They said "Isn't that nice." They gave me fifty dollars and showed me the hospital where Durwood would be which was very pretty too with a little pond in the front of it and the dog rode in the car with us and licked my face and I loved those old people and asked them to take me with them. And they said "Here's your bus," and I got on it. (*The two sisters hold each other's hands. Captain Holahan puts down the phone. Lights up. Rosalie goes into the dark.*)

HOLAHAN. We called the Peach family, honey.

BETTY. Don't call me honey. Okay?

HOLAHAN. They told us you were there.

BETTY. So I'm free. Alibis.

HOLAHAN. Honey, you don't need alibis for South Carolina. You need alibis for Bleecker Street. That's the required address of your alibis, honey. You could've killed Bert before you left so you wouldn't miss out on a joy ride to southern climes. Your boy putting cramps deep in your life style. The Peach family of Solomon Ferry don't tell me nothing. The main event we're conferring about took place in New York City. (*Rosalie appears L. The piano plays melodramatically. Lights out on Betty and Holahan. Rosalie appears R., by piano. She speaks excitedly, like one of those action-news reporters covering a live event. She remains on stage for the following scenes.*)

ROSALIE. Scenes containing information the police would never know. Scenes containing information the mother would never know, never could know. (*Bert and Donny appear. Bert is flashing some of Durwood's money.*)

BERT. Hey, Donny my man.

DONNY. Hey Mr. Bert my man.

BERT. Want to see what I got? Not so close.

DONNY. You want to sneak into monosodium glutamate?

BERT. What's your mouth talking, my man?

DONNY. M.S.G. That's what rock musicians call Madison Square Garden. Monosodium glutamate. You know the stuff they put in Chinese restaurants that makes your face go all measles? You want to sneak in there tonight?

BERT. To a Chinese restaurant?

DONNY. To Madison Square Garden? They got hockey or a concert or a flower show.

BERT. My man, if I go to monosodium glutamate, I go walking right in the front door paying my own way. (*Bert takes out a bill.*)
DONNY. Where'd you get a ten? You pulling jobs yourself? Hey, I'm the man with the monkey. You into money now by yourself? You deal me in. I got the dibs on the monkey.
BERT. No jobs by myself.
DONNY. You dealing? Coke? Pills? Is that more bills in there? They counterfeit?
BERT. No, my man. They are real as a summer's day.
DONNY. Bullshit. Those are counterfeit. That's play money.
BERT. You want to see? We go into the bank. (*Lights up on a bank counter. The teller stands behind it. The music continues.*)
ROSALIE. They go into the bank on Sheridan Square. They wait in line.
BERT. (*To teller.*) My man, is this bill negotiable? What I'm saying is there's no doubt about the accuracy of this denominational piece of merchandise. (*The teller takes the proferred bill and holds it up to the light.*)
DONNY. They got a sign in the A & P saying beware ten dollar bills being circulated. (*The teller smiles and hands the bill back.*)
BERT. It's real? There's no doubts? And if I had more with serial numbers right in line, they'd all be real too? Thank you, my man. Here's a quarter. A tip for your appraisal.
ROSALIE. They walk away from the bank clerk. The bank is crowded. (*Bert goes L. to a glass desk in the bank.*)
BERT. Come here. I want to do something. It's a funny joke I saw about a bank. You take—anybody looking? —a deposit slip and you write on the back: Hand over all your money or I blow your brains on the wall.
DONNY. Where'd you get that money?
BERT. Then you put the deposit slip back where it came from.
DONNY. Come on. Tell.
BERT. Then you wait. (*Raulito enters the bank area. He takes a deposit slip. He fills it out. Goes to the teller, who takes the deposit slip. The teller looks around panicky. He pushes a button. A siren. Gun shots. Raulito looks around, his chest covered with blood. Blood comes out of his mouth.*)
RAULITO. I come into the bank to make deposit number seventeen in the Christmas Club. Time to make deposit number Seventeen. Christmas Club. (*He falls. His trench coat opens. His*

evening gown trembles down. He falls against the counter. Lights out. Music up.)

DONNY. Buy me something. Your money's burning holes in my pockets. Let's go.

ROSALIE. They go. (*The stage is bare. Joanne has joined Bert and Donny. The three of them walk in circles. Bert is busy, focused in.*)

DONNY. (*To Joanne.*) Hey, Joanne, Bert's crazy. You know what he's doing? Putting razor blades in frisbees and then when we see somebody we don't like from Elizabeth Irwin High School, we toss it at them and say "Hey, grab!"

JOANNE. Papers I read a German shepherd ate a new born baby.

BERT. Shut up, Joanne.

DONNY. Bert's mother's been gone two days now. She left him a lot of money.

JOANNE. The mother went out and left the baby for a moment and the dog ate the baby.

BERT. Shut up, Joanne. You're a real creep. My mother's right. You're a walking exorcism picture. All the time you're so creepy.

JOANNE. Your mother likes me.

BERT. She says you give her the creeps.

DONNY. Momma's boy.

BERT. I'm not!

JOANNE. You are so.

BERT. I like my mother being away. I got the apartment to myself. I'm eating good. Boy, my mother's a rotten cook. I see those commercials Food like mother used to make. I say Boy, that's the worst commercial God ever made.

JOANNE. Momma's boy.

BERT. Shut up. There's the restaurant where the bicycle got my aunt.

DONNY. What kind of bicycle?

BERT. Ten-speed Raleigh. Yellow.

JOANNE. You got the money. You could buy a ten-speed Raleigh yellow. If you weren't so chintzy.

BERT. No way. Money's got to last me.

DONNY. She was a nice lady.

BERT. That's how we came down to New York from Maine. We had her funeral then we stayed and stayed. Wasn't for that ten-speed Raleigh whizzing around the corner, we'd still be in Maine.

48

JOANNE. Momma's boy.

DONNY. Where's your father? My mother says how come we never see Bert's father?

BERT. He's away on secret duty.

JOANNE. Oh sure.

BERT. He's on the payroll of foreign governments. He calls me all the time and asks me not to tell where he is because if it got out.

JOANNE. Oh sure.

DONNY. The CIA?

BERT. More secret than the CIA.

JOANNE. Nothing is more secret than the CIA.

BERT. If it's such a good secret then how come you know about the CIA. The place my father works for is so secret it don't have no name or initials or nothing.

JOANNE. Or existence. (*Calls in distance:*) Hey, Margie? Want to sneak in to what's playing at the Greenwhich? The Waverly? I don't care. (*Joanne goes.*)

BERT. What a creep.

DONNY. German shepherds are gonna eat her some day.

BERT. Suppose one day your money runs out and you don't know anybody, what do you do?

DONNY. You work.

BERT. Fourteen you can't work. They put you in orphanages? You go to the police, they arrest you? What do you do?

DONNY. You got all this money.

BERT. Suppose it runs out.

DONNY. Thousand dollars don't run out.

BERT. Sure it can.

DONNY. You sure you got it?

BERT. You want to see it? (*They run. Music plays. Threatening. Blackness. Then one spotlight shining down at C. They're in Bert's apartment.*) Hello?

DONNY. You think there's anybody here?

BERT. Ma?

DONNY. Is she here? (*Bert runs in and out of the light.*)

BERT. I hid the money behind the curtains. I hid the money in the toilet. I hid the money in the freezer. I hid the money under the bed. I hid the money in the oven. I hid the money under the carpet. I hid the money in the shower. I hid the money in our shoes. I hid the money in pockets of clothes we don't wear. I hid the money. (*Bert's arms are filled with the bills.*) How long can it last me? Suppose somebody comes in the window? Suppose they steal the money? Who am I gonna call? It's not me. It's a friend. I'm talking about a friend. What if my friend gets locked out? How will he get back in? Is there an earthquake? Why is the room shaking? I can't stop shaking? Hold down the floor! I don't know where she is! She went away and left me! She went out the door! She left me! She went away! I'm turning to water! My stomach's coming up! The floor is moving! (*He hugs Donny.*)

DONNY. (*Pause.*) Hey. Don't you hug me. Hey. You don't touch me. You hear me? You get your mitts off me. You hear.

BERT. I'm going away. Hang on to me.

DONNY. You keep your hands to yourself. You keep your hands. It was your idea bringing those guys up here and hitting them. You the one that brought them up. You brought up too many. You got too many watches, Bert. You stay away from me.

BERT. Suppose she never comes back?

DONNY. (*Takes out his monkey wrench.*) I know what this is. You brought me up here to get my watches, didn't you. You earned all that money. You brought me up here. You're doing recruiting for those old guys down at the docks who want kids.

BERT. Suppose she don't ever come back. (*Bert clutches Donny around his knees. Donny lifts his monkey wrench over Bert's head. They freeze. Rosalie appears.*)

ROSALIE. And all the dead people, the people who have died, me, Raulito, Durwood, the Dope King of Providence, Mavis Brennan, the man on the ten-speed bike, all the dead people in our lives join together and lead Donny to the wrench and put his hands around the wrench and lead the wrench to Bert's head and we hold Bert's head so Donny can bring the wrench down onto Bert's head with greater ease. Bert falls. Donny takes the thousand dollars. And at this time precisely, Betty was being put on a Greyhound bus at Crossroads Corner, South Carolina and being sent back to New York. Betty turns around in the window and sees the parents of Durwood and Durwood's wife waving goodbye. (*Joanne runs into the apartment area. She knocks on the door.*)

JOANNE. Bert? Donny?

DONNY. Go away.

JOANNE. You in there?

DONNY. Get out of here, Joanne.

JOANNE. I'm coming in.

DONNY. You stay outside there.

JOANNE. I just got a summer job.

DONNY. Don't come in.

JOANNE. Checkout girl at the A & P. (*Joanne is trying to push the door in. Donny is trying to hold it shut. Joanne pushes the door in. Donny falls back.*) You got to be very strong to be a checkout girl at the *A & P*.

DONNY. You tell and I'll.

JOANNE. (*After walking around and around Bert.*) That's what a dead person looks like?

DONNY. He made me do it.

JOANNE. All the time you read about dead people and hear about dead people but this is my first. Not embalmed or anything.

DONNY. He tried to touch me.

JOANNE. Just regular dead.

DONNY. He put his hands on me.

JOANNE. I'm glad it's Bert. I'd hate my first dead person to be a stranger.

DONNY. I'm not ever going to not believe in dreams again. I dreamed the other night and the night before that and once about six months ago that a yellow checker cab stopped and a man got out and dragged me in and when the cab stopped we were in a quiet warehouse so you could look down and see the river and waiting in a line was all these men with drool coming out of their mouths and my feet were in cement and the old man touched me only he wasn't old anymore and that dream came true just now. Bert was the old man. My feet were in cement. I am not going to end up my life in any dream. I stopped that dream. Anybody tells you dreams don't tell the future you send them to me. (*Joanne holds Donny.*)

JOANNE. We'll say somebody killed him.

DONNY. Who killed him?

JOANNE. One of those guys you bring up here with the watches.

DONNY. I don't want any part of it. Cops up here. They'll find fingerprints.

JOANNE. Okay. They've had all those murders down at the docks. We'll put Bert in a bag and bring him down the river and leave him there. By the warehouse.

DONNY. But those murders. The school crossing lady told me

51

those bodies—they had no heads. The maniac takes the heads off.

JOANNE. You got a saw?

DONNY. There's one out there.

JOANNE. You start cutting. Put papers down.

DONNY. Is this a crime!

JOANNE. He's all ready dead. You're making a mess.

DONNY. My uncle saw a dirty movie and he told me Bert's mother was in it. (*They take Bert by the feet and drag him into the dark.*)

JOANNE. Bert wasn't from here. Bert never belonged here. (*They are gone. Rosalie steps forward. Betty appears in light, R. at a phone. She dials.*)

ROSALIE. Betty is now in Washington, D. C. She roams around Washington D. C. looking at monuments. She buys a dress to calm herself. She calls Bert at a pay phone. (*The phone rings. Lights up on apartment. Donny and Joanne come into the overhead light area.*)

JOANNE. Don't get it.

DONNY. It might be for me.

JOANNE. Don't get it. I'll wait for you outside. (*Lights out on Donny and Joanne and Betty.*)

ROSALIE. Betty hangs up. She walks to the Capital building to look for the Declaration of Independence she saw printed on parchment paper like the original. She will bring it home to Bert for a present. (*Lights up at C. to signify street.*)

DONNY. I'm finished. I put him in a duffle bag. (*The two of them drag the bag.*)

JOANNE. Here's a shopping cart.

DONNY. We can't steal that. The A & P arrests you.

JOANNE. I'm going to be working there this summer. Employees are allowed to use them. (*They load Bert's body in the bag into the cart. They begin pushing.*)

DONNY. You can smell the river tonight. (*Margie comes up.*)

MARGIE. Hi. Joanne, could I talk to you.

JOANNE. Go away, Margie.

MARGIE. I got to talk to you.

JOANNE. Later Margie.

MARGIE. What's in there?

DONNY. Margie, I believe Joanne was talking to you.

MARGIE. I want to see what you're pushing.

JOANNE. My grandmother's dog died and we're going to bury it in the river.

MARGIE. Can I walk with you? I don't want to go home yet. My mother's watching television. My father's kicking ass in the living room. I got to talk to somebody. Something happened to me this afternoon. Joanne, I got to talk to you. Something is happening to my body. My body starts changing and I don't like it. It's like it's a sin what's happening to my body. I keep going to confession and confessing that things are happening to my body and the priest says but that's growing up and I say I don't want to grow up. Those things that are happening to me have got to be sins. I want to grow up so I can leave home and get a job and make some money and get a record player and get married but I want my body to stop what it's doing. What kind of dog was it?

DONNY. I don't like it down here.

JOANNE. Look at the yellow cabs. People pulling up. Going into those warehouses. People climbing into those trucks.

DONNY. It's like my dream. (*The cart tips over. Bert's head rolls out. Margie screams. Donny puts it back in the bag. Joanne takes Margie's hands. She and Donny put Margie's hands in the bag.*)

JOANNE. You're part of this forever and ever. You're part of it.

MARGIE. I'm out taking a walk.

DONNY. Here's money. Don't tell.

JOANNE. Shut up, Donny.

MARGIE. Where'd you get that money?

JOANNE. Don't give it to her.

DONNY. She'll tell.

JOANNE. She won't.

MARGIE. I got to go home!

JOANNE. You are a part of this.

MARGIE. I never saw nothing. My brain is dead. You hear me? I swear? My eyes are blind. I was never out. My ears don't hear. My brain is dead. I'm just out taking a walk. My brain don't register nothing. My eyes don't see. Forever. I'm never seeing nothing. Please. I'll see you. Later. School. I'll see you tomorrow. That's all. (*Donny and Joanne push the cart into the darkness. There is a splash. Darkness. Rosalie steps forward. The piano plays "Hey, Stay a While," very bouncily, cheery. Rosalie does the stripper's walk while talking to us in the audience.*)

ROSALIE. So Betty returned to New York, called Raulito to make sure her job was still safe with Honeymoon Holidays and to make a wonderful joke about her southern adventure of the past few days and she smiled because she would make it sound funny like a wonderful guest on the Johnny Carson show. Some Cuban relative answered the phone and told her Raulito was dead, shot while trying to hold up the Chase Manhattan Bank. Betty laughed till she realized a truth was being told. She ran home and found police waiting there and when they told her Bert was dead, her son was dead, for a moment got Bert and Raulito mixed up in her head. They both couldn't be dead. She had this picture that her apartment had become a branch of Chase Manhattan and that's what Raulito was holding up. They took her down to the morgue and she asked why her son was on two tables. One large and one small. She identified his body. She identified his head. The room was identical to the one she had identified her sister in two years ago and somehow that comforted her, that she had been here before. She did not know, Betty, nor would she ever know that two drawers over from her son's was Raulito's body. Betty was taken into custody. Betty was questioned for a long time. Betty was released. Months went by. A summer. Joanne and Donny were very nice to her for a while but kids get new friends and kids forget and Betty hardly ever saw Bert's friends anymore. She draws a circle on a map and sees an island forty miles off the coast of Massachusetts is the furthest she can get away from New York, from the mainland with the sixty odd dollars she has in her account. She gives up the apartment. She takes the bus to Massachusetts. She steps onto the ferry. She looks at the houses of great families on the shore. She talks with a man of quintuplets born many years ago. Talk of family and children. The sea is autumn calm. Seagulls fly above. (*The music stops. This stage is filled with light. We are on the deck of the boat as at the beginning. Holahan and Betty appear at the ship railing. Rosalie goes into black.*)

HOLAHAN. You recognized me?

BETTY. Captain Marvin Holahan. Sixth Precinct Homicide. (*Holahan pulls off his disguise.*)

HOLAHAN. What did you write in that note? (*She throws sheets of small papers into the wind. They blow away. She pours bottles overboard.*)

BETTY. A confession. A full confession. I wrote down everything that happened. And it's all gone. There it goes. There's your case.

HOLAHAN. I got bounced. From the force. About six days after our meeting. I took a lot out on you. I was on probation at the time of that interrogation. I had a lot of secret pressures on me. I thought if I nailed you, they'd overlook this minor nothing drug bribe extortion rap they pinned on me which if the truth be known everybody on the force is involved with in one way or another. But they were looking for a patsy. I loved the way you stood up to me. I wanted you to be the killer. If I stayed on the force I would've found your boy's killer.

BETTY. No matter. I got on the bus this morning and I started writing on little pieces of paper everything I ever knew. Everything that ever happened to me. Sentences. Places. People's names. Secrets. Things I wanted to be. I thought maybe out of all that I'd find the magic clue who killed my kid. I'd say I see.

HOLAHAN. I tried to do investigations on my own to find the killer for a present to you. But you can't investigate outside the force. You need that power. You need . . . that secret power the force offers.

BETTY. It bothered me at first not knowing who killed Bert. But then I thought of all the things we don't know. All the secrets in the world got put in a bottle and thrown in the sea and maybe someday I'll be walking along a beach and the bottle containing the message for me will wash up. If I don't know the answer, it's out there and one day maybe an incredible coincidence will occur and I'll know all I need to know. Or the murderer will come forward. Or I'll even forget once I had a secret. I'll remember I had a boy like I'll remember I once had a mother and once had a father and I'll try to keep piling the weight on to the present, so I'll stay alive and won't slide back. If I don't know, somebody knows. My life is a triumph of all the things I don't know. I don't have to know everything. I read Agatha Christie's and throw them away when the detective says "And the murderer is . . ." The mystery's always greater than the solution. I was terrified to have a kid. I said before I got pregnant I'll have a kid and the eyes will end up on one side of the face and all the fingers on one hand and all the toes on one foot and both ears on one side of the head. And Bert was born and he was perfect. And this is the only thing I know. There's got to be some order in there. I'm moving to this new place and it has big houses with classical columns and maybe I'll find a job in one of them in a house owned by an old man who has an art collection

55

and I'll read up on classical painters and maybe he'll ask me to marry him or maybe I'll kill him and get him to sign the collection over to me or maybe I'll love him and marry him. Or maybe I'll discover a secret inside me that will make the whole world better. I'm not discounting nothing. Maybe I'll be transplanted into somebody great who knows the secret, my secret, or maybe I'll never know and a tornado or a water spout will whisk me up and I'll turn into rain and end up in that sea.

HOLAHAN. All I know is I know more about you than anyone I know. All those months doing dossiers on you. All disconnected. All disjointed. Still I know more about you. We both have to begin again. Maybe together? I could reveal myself to you slowly. That was not me who interrogated you. That was my job talking. That was unseen pressures talking to you. That was saving my skin talking to you. I feel for you. All what you've been through. I feel for you. I read stories people falling in love who threw acid in each other's faces and they get out of prison and they still love each other. I read stories people try to kill each other and end up loving each other. Give me a chance? I got severence pay? I got enough to get us through a winter? (*She looks at him fearfully. She turns. Rosalie appears* L. *Piano plays* "Voices of Eagles" *very simply under the dialogue. Holahan steps into dark.*)

ROSALIE. Last scene. In which Betty remembers the conversation she and I had so many years ago, the intensity of it burned into the Good Humor man's head. Betty has tried to remember since that day what Rosalie, what I had told her. She remembers. She and I sat on a summer afternoon on the green porch steps. Our mother over there. Our father over there. We pulled our skirts over our legs. (*Betty and Rosalie stand side by side as young girls.*) Stop shaking. Don't let them see. (*The parents.*) It's nothing, Dad.

BETTY. It's like my stomach's going to come up all the time.

ROSALIE. You're all right.

BETTY. How am I going to get through my life?

ROSALIE. Would you let me explain? Our spirits—it's so simple —float around in space and it all makes sense when you realize the planet Earth has these fishing hooks on it. What we call gravity is fishing hooks and all the nice things in the world are baited on those hooks and our spirits floating up there all loose and aimless spy those baited hooks and we bite. And we are reeled down onto this planet and we spend the rest of our stay on this planet trying to free our mouths of that hook, fighting, fighting.

BETTY. But what do you do?

ROSALIE. You travel alone because other people are only there to remind you how much that hook hurts that we all bit down on. Wait for that one day we can bite free and get back out there in space where we belong, sail back over water, over skies, into space, the hook finally out of our mouths and we wander back out there in space spawning to other planets never to return hurrah to earth and we'll look back and can't even see these lives here anymore. Only the taste of blood to remind us we ever existed. The earth is small. We're gone. We're dead. We're safe.

BETTY. But momma says—

ROSALIE. Oh, momma says. Momma says. When are you gonna think for yourself?

BETTY. How do you . . . How can I think for myself? (*Rosalie has no answer. Bells ring.*) Vanilla? You want vanilla? We hear you, Durwood! (*Rosalie runs off. Betty turns. Holahan is there, having moved into the light. Betty considers Holahan. A long pause. She moves to him. The move turns into two actors bowing to the audience. Lights out. Music plays. Company bow.*)

Production Notes

John Wulp designed *Landscape of the Body* in its world premiere performance at the Academy Festival Theatre, in Lake Forest, Illinois, after a rehearsal period at the New York Shakespeare Festival in New York, the theatre to which the production would return. Wulp's central image of the play was of a series of black boxes from which people entered and exited as if in a dream. I loved this conception for making manifest the central theme in the play: people fighting against the death in all our lives. The play would then be surrounded by light, a great whiteness, in its beginning and end scenes on the steamer to Nantucket. Laura Crow's costumes would have a bright iridescent shimmer against the black. Jennifer Tipton's light would sculpt out of this void. John Wulp designed two concentric turntables and on either side of them two smaller turntables.

In these production notes I can only say, keep the production as simple as possible. Have *Rosalie* over there on Stage Left with her piano and accompanist. Have the opening as bright and exhilarating as possible. Capture the zest when journeys begin. Have the center of the play move in and out of darkness where dreams and memories and mindless violence can take their turn.

J.G.

PROPERTY LIST

ACT ONE

Note paper and pen (Betty)
Shopping bags, with bottles
Suitcase
False nose, with eyeglasses (Holahan)
Desk and chairs ⎫ (for Police Station)
Desk lamp ⎭
Pills (*Tums*) in pocket (Betty)
Earphone radio (Bert)
Wristwatches (Donny)
Box of chocolates
Piano
Sink ⎫
Kitchen table, with coffee cups ⎪
Chairs ⎪
Day bed ⎬ (for Rosalie's apartment)
Bean bag chair ⎪
Vanity table, with make-up materials ⎭
Broken bicycle
TV set
Dress, in paper bag (Betty)
Wristwatches (Bert)
Butterfly pin (Betty)
Telephone ⎫
Telephone books ⎪
Newspapers ⎪ (for Travel
Desk and chairs ⎬ Agency)
Tape machine, with cassettes (cheering and applause) ⎭
Plates of food
Bouquet of flowers ⎫
Snapshots ⎪
Note ⎬ (Durwood)
Wad of folding money ⎭
Cigarettes and matches (Dope King)
Marijuana "joints"
Basin and pitcher of water
Shampoo

Act Two

Desk
Chairs
Telephone
Money (Bert)
Bank counter, with deposit slips
Bank counter, for teller
Money, in apartment area
Monkey wrench
Pay phone
Duffle bag
Grocery cart
"Bert's head"

HEY, STAY A WHILE

♩=72-80

HEY, STAY A WHILE IN THE CROOK OF MY ARMS.

ALL YOU GOT TO DO____ IS LOOK IN MY ARMS AND YOU'LL

SEE HOME SWEET HOME.____ I'LL IN-VEST IN A DOOR-MAT.____

SIT BACK, RE— LAX, COOL BROW, TEN-SION SLACKS.

HEY, STAY A WHILE. —— MY ARMS ARE FILLED WITH WHAT THE WHOLE WORLD

LACKS. HEY STAY A WHILE. ——

MR. RIGHT

(WARN:) BICYCLIST. "CHOCOLATE KISSES"

(CUE:) WHEN PIANO T.T. STARTS REVOLVE

BRITE 4

THAT MIS-TER RIGHT! IF IT WAS ILL LET IT PASS. THAT

Play Ricky-Tic Bar Room Style Like Intro

RIGHT MIS-TER RIGHT THAT FUNNY LOOK-IN', SKUNK PYT ME KER-

PLUNK ON MY ASS. I THOUGHT MIS-TER RIGHT WOULD HAVE A LITTLE MORE

COUTH HE'D COME ON A WHITE CHARG-ER. SAY HI-DE-

HI TO MY CHARM AND VO- DE- OH TO MY YOUTH!
G [PLAY RICKY-TIC UNDER DIALOGUE   G7

C

G   B7   Em7

A7   D   D7   GLISS

LATIN VAMP
G   F/D   G   F/D   etc----

PLAY LATIN STYLE UNTIL (CUE:) RAULITO: "FOLLOW THE LEADER."
STOP

V.S.

FRIGHTENED OF YOU

ROSALIE:
FRIGHT-ENED OF YOU

ALL OF THESE YEARS ___ NE-VER SE-CURE ___ IN YOUR EM-BRACE

SLEEP THROUGH THE NIGHT ___ DREAM THAT I'M DEAD ___

WHAT'S GETTING ME THROUGH MY LIFE? __ WHAT'S MY EX-CUSE IN — SIDE? __

WHAT'S KEEPING ME IN MY LIFE? __ THE MOLE-HILL OF LUST OR THE MOUN-TAIN OF PRIDE? __

FOR-GIVE ME MY DEAR __

SLIP OF THE TONGUE __ FOR — GET WHAT I SAID __ E — RASE __

68

DON'T HIT ME _____ I LOVE YOU _____

A LITTLE TOMORROW

(WARN:) BERT: "THE BROOM CLOSET"

(CUE:) THEY LIGHT JOINTS
PIANO J.T STARTS REVOLVE

LITTLE TOMORROW - 3.

YES-TER-

G/D   G+/D#   E⁷ G+/D# G/D   A9/C#   C/D

[VAMP]

DAYS

mf

←PLAY UNTIL PIANO TURNTABLE REVOLVES BACK

VOICES OF EAGLES

♩=60   [BERT.]

I USED TO BE-LIEVE WHEN I WAS YOUNG

I UN-DER-STOOD EV-'RY NOTE THAT WAS SUNG. VOI-CES OF SPAR-ROWS, VOI-CES OF BLUE JAYS,

rit - - - - - [TEMPO]

VOI-CES OF RO-BINS, VOI-CES OF EA-GLES. WHEN I WAS YOUNG I USED TO PRE-TEND THROUGH

I USED TO BE-LIEVE WHEN I WAS YOUNG I UN-DER-STOOD EV-RY NOTE THAT WAS SUNG. _____ VOI-CES OF EA-GLES. _____

NEW PLAYS

★ **SHEL'S SHORTS by Shel Silverstein.** Lauded poet, songwriter and author of children's books, the incomparable Shel Silverstein's short plays are deeply infused with the same wicked sense of humor that made him famous. "...[a] childlike honesty and twisted sense of humor." *–Boston Herald.* "...terse dialogue and an absurdity laced with a tang of dread give [*Shel's Shorts*] more than a trace of Samuel Beckett's comic existentialism." *–Boston Phoenix.* [flexible casting] ISBN: 0-8222-1897-6

★ **AN ADULT EVENING OF SHEL SILVERSTEIN by Shel Silverstein.** Welcome to the darkly comic world of Shel Silverstein, a world where nothing is as it seems and where the most innocent conversation can turn menacing in an instant. These ten imaginative plays vary widely in content, but the style is unmistakable. "...[*An Adult Evening*] shows off Silverstein's virtuosic gift for wordplay...[and] sends the audience out...with a clear appreciation of human nature as perverse and laughable." *–NY Times.* [flexible casting] ISBN: 0-8222-1873-9

★ **WHERE'S MY MONEY? by John Patrick Shanley.** A caustic and sardonic vivisection of the institution of marriage, laced with the author's inimitable razor-sharp wit. "...Shanley's gift for acid-laced one-liners and emotionally tumescent exchanges is certainly potent..." *–Variety.* "...lively, smart, occasionally scary and rich in reverse wisdom." *–NY Times.* [3M, 3W] ISBN: 0-8222-1865-8

★ **A FEW STOUT INDIVIDUALS by John Guare.** A wonderfully screwy comedy-drama that figures Ulysses S. Grant in the throes of writing his memoirs, surrounded by a cast of fantastical characters, including the Emperor and Empress of Japan, the opera star Adelina Patti and Mark Twain. "Guare's smarts, passion and creativity skyrocket to awesome heights..." *–Star Ledger.* "...precisely the kind of good new play that you might call an everyday miracle...every minute of it is fresh and newly alive..." *–Village Voice.* [10M, 3W] ISBN: 0-8222-1907-7

★ **BREATH, BOOM by Kia Corthron.** A look at fourteen years in the life of Prix, a Bronx native, from her ruthless girl-gang leadership at sixteen through her coming to maturity at thirty. "...vivid world, believable and eye-opening, a place worthy of a dramatic visit, where no one would want to live but many have to." *–NY Times.* "...rich with humor, terse vernacular strength and gritty detail..." *–Variety.* [1M, 9W] ISBN: 0-8222-1849-6

★ **THE LATE HENRY MOSS by Sam Shepard.** Two antagonistic brothers, Ray and Earl, are brought together after their father, Henry Moss, is found dead in his seedy New Mexico home in this classic Shepard tale. "...His singular gift has been for building mysteries out of the ordinary ingredients of American family life..." *–NY Times.* "...rich moments ...Shepard finds gold." *–LA Times.* [7M, 1W] ISBN: 0-8222-1858-5

★ **THE CARPETBAGGER'S CHILDREN by Horton Foote.** One family's history spanning from the Civil War to WWII is recounted by three sisters in evocative, intertwining monologues. "...bittersweet music—[a] rhapsody of ambivalence...in its modest, garrulous way...theatrically daring." *–The New Yorker.* [3W] ISBN: 0-8222-1843-7

★ **THE NINA VARIATIONS by Steven Dietz.** In this funny, fierce and heartbreaking homage to *The Seagull*, Dietz puts Chekhov's star-crossed lovers in a room and doesn't let them out. "A perfect little jewel of a play..." *–Shepherdstown Chronicle.* "...a delightful revelation of a writer at play; and also an odd, haunting, moving theater piece of lingering beauty." *–Eastside Journal (Seattle).* [1M, 1W (flexible casting)] ISBN: 0-8222-1891-7

DRAMATISTS PLAY SERVICE, INC.
440 Park Avenue South, New York, NY 10016 212-683-8960 Fax 212-213-1539
postmaster@dramatists.com www.dramatists.com